The
ULTIMATE WEDDING
RECEPTION BOOK

Plan it, Do it, Love it!

Here's How...

Bill Cox
With
Janie Franz

Table of Contents

PREFACE

This book is an easy step-by-step guide that will help brides, grooms, and their parents plan the perfect wedding reception. The tips found here may also be useful to wedding planners.

Over the past eleven years, I have been a mobile DJ and have worked over a thousand–actually 1,176 and counting, at this writing-wedding receptions. I have developed a wedding reception sequence that will relieve some of the stresses of wedding receptions and will create a flowing order of events that the wedding reception hosts will be proud of. It doesn't matter whether it's a small, intimate $2,000 affair or a large, spare-no-expense $200,000 to $2+ million wedding reception. These techniques will work no matter what amount you spend on your wedding. After all, no amount of money can buy an embarrassment-free event.

Couples spend a lot of time anticipating the wedding day, the wedding ceremony, and the wedding reception. Here in American society, people don't talk about going to the wedding or "It was a great wedding." They are more likely to talk about the party afterwards, the wedding reception. Weddings are formal, religious or civil, ceremonies that create a bond between a man and a woman. The true celebration begins when the couple entertains for the first time at the wedding reception. In today's society, people need to be entertained, to feel that they are part of the party. Through the wedding reception sequence that I have developed, I have found a way that will help couples maximize the amount of time and money that they put into their wedding reception.

Many times when I consult with brides and grooms in the planning stages, they'll tell me what's important is that they have a great party. Of course, they want to have the highlights of the wedding reception accented and have them documented through reception photos, the mementoes of that occasion. Ultimately, though, they want to have fun doing that, and they want to make sure that their friends have a good time. Now, a lot of that has to do with keeping the guests' interest, making sure that they stay and then participate and have fun doing it. And what that depends upon is the flow of the event itself.

I feel that a wedding reception has specific formalities that must be adhered to, and those formalities must be documented. All of this must be done in a timely and orderly fashion. I feel that by using the formula that I will lay out in this book, you will be able to honor the bridal couple and have all of the traditional pictures for your wedding album. Plus, you'll have plenty of time to visit with your guests and have fun doing it.

There are very few books out there solely about wedding receptions, and that's why I'm writing this one–not to be on the New York Times bestseller list. If you are a young couple with very little resources and are paying for your wedding yourself or your family is very well heeled and footing the bill for it all, ultimately I want to help you maximize the money that you spend on your wedding reception and make sure that you have the time of your life. Nothing would make me feel more honored than to have someone buy a copy of this book, read it, and pass it to her friend, and then to have her friend pass it to her friend, and on and on. All brides deserve "The Ultimate Wedding Reception." I offer this book as a humble guide.

– Bill Cox

Dedicated to the Trinity of Faith, Family and Friends; for without one, life itself would not be possible.

– Bill Cox

INTRODUCTION

Why a Wedding Reception

Despite dismal marriage statistics, couples are continuing to get married well into the twenty-first century. The institution of marriage is so valued that once a couple splits up, each partner often remarries, sometimes repeating the process more than once. Each time, the new marriage is witnessed and legalized through religious or civil ceremonies. Wedding receptions nearly always follow. Why do the couples' parents or the couples themselves put on a party after tying the knot?

Historically, there have been wedding feasts in nearly every culture, and sometimes those parties were far more elaborate and more drawn out than the formal rites sealing a couple's lives together. The Bible tells of Jacob and Samson enjoying their wedding celebrations for seven days. Then, there's the well-known story of Jesus being persuaded by his mother to help with the wine when the supply had long been depleted and the guests were still partying at his cousin's wedding. Jesus avoided embarrassment to his host by converting water to wine.

The ancient Greeks used to throw a big feast for every wedded couple. What was so special about those parties was that women were always invited to them and were excluded from every other festive occasion.

One thing is certain. A wedding reception honors the newly-married couple and the people who are closest to them—their parents and those in the wedding party. We also document traditional events at the wedding reception by pho-tographing the cutting of the cake, the toast, and the tossing of the bouquet and the garter. The wedding couple may also par-ticipate in other traditions according to their family back-grounds or ethnicities. With the changing face of today's bride due to delaying first marriages and subsequent remar-riages (the average age is 25 for first marriages with senior citizen brides becoming more numerous also), there may be many other traditions added to the wedding reception. Some brides are including their children from previous marriages in special reception events or are honoring previous in-laws in various ways.

Basically, there are three kinds of wedding receptions. One is the simple reception, usually at the site of the wedding ceremony. It is merely an eat-and-greet affair with the cake cutting as a highlight.

Another is the reception at either the site of the wedding or at a hall or club with a separate wedding dance held at a lo-cal drinking establishment. The separate wedding dance is a phenomenon of weddings in the Northern Plains and may have grown out of small towns that had no facilities for a re-ception and dance in one location. The couple could eat at the church and cut the cake. Then regroup with the wedding party afterwards at the local bar to dance. The couple paid for a keg for the whole bar or just paid for the band for the night. Notices were put out in the newspaper, and the whole town would come out to dance and honor the couple.

The most common after-nuptials celebration is the recep-tion and dance in one location, usually at a hall, country club, or banquet facility. Though any or all of the techniques that I illustrate in this book can be applied to any type of wedding reception, the reception/dance is the one that I am most familiar with and incorporates all of the tips that I suggest. It is also the one that all of the bridal magazines and books talk about. It is the one that most of us have attended on one occasion or another and have come away either having had a great time or been totally embarrassed for the wedding couple and/or reception hosts. It is, therefore, critical to plan your reception well so that everyone has fun and you (and your parents) shine as social wizards.

EARLY DECISIONS

Planning a wedding reception may seem like a daunting task. Some brides have never even throw a party before. Others may have just called up a few friends and supplied a couple of bottles of wine. A few may have organized an event in college or helped an older sister or cousin plan her wedding. Few have the experience of ordering food for several hundred guests and orchestrating their entertainment. Even a small affair of twenty people has its own task list and order of events. That is one reason to enlist the help of other people, including the groom, your parents, and your bridesmaids and groomsmen. I think that may be one reason why the wedding party exists, at least today, to help the bride.

ORIGINS OF THE WEDDING PARTY

There are two stories that illustrate how the wedding party may have come about. In ancient Egypt, it was thought that weddings attracted evil spirits who wanted to spoil the joyous occasion. In order to confuse the evil spirits and to protect the bride, several women from the bride's family would dress exactly like the bride and accompanied the bride to the wedding. The bride also carried a bouquet of scented herbs and flowers to help ward off the spirits.

The other story says that the origins of the bridal party was in medieval times when a young man saw a young lady whom he wanted for his wife and carried her off to his home or to the church. The women in the bride's family would gather around her and protect her from the groom. Later, they began to dress exactly like the bride in order to confuse him. The groom also brought his best friend to help fight off the maiden's brothers. As brides began to collect more female helpers, grooms also brought more friends to help him. Both the bride and the groom eventually had groups of family and friends surrounding them, all dressed similarly. The women also began wearing veils to confuse the groom further. This tradition continued into Victorian England. Soon, the bridal abduction became a high-spirited tradition that was part of a more formal ceremony and celebration.

The groom also put the bride on his left side so that he could use his sword hand to fend off the bride's family. That is why the bride is on the left in most wedding ceremonies.

Though you are asking for help from your family and friends, you must remember that this is your wedding—yours and your grooms. Whatever decisions you make must make you both happy. Wedding receptions, remember, are the first formal parties that a bride and groom give for their friends and family. It's the first time you entertain as a married couple. You want to make people feel comfortable and you want to share your joy with them. By all means, accommodate some of each family's suggestions, but you don't have to let Aunt Agnes sing at your reception or hire the caterer that Grandma likes, if you don't want to. And don't include anything that you feel you can't afford or don't feel comfortable doing. Create your own traditions through your own wedding planning.

This is critical if you are an encore bride. It is difficult enough to respect everyone's wishes when you are trying to accommodate two families (the bride's and the groom's), but it is impossible to accommodate the wishes of six or more families (the bride's parents who may be divorced and bringing new spouses, the groom's parents who may be divorced and bringing new spouses, the bride's children, the groom's children, the bride's in-laws who are her children's grandparents, and the groom's in-laws who are his children's grandparents—and maybe even the ex-spouses and their new husbands and wives). A remarriage today has become a tribal celebration, except that it is not confined to one village but exists in a global community. By all means, include all of the people who are close to you; just create a celebration that brings those people together to share your joy. After all, a wedding reception reflects the style and spirit of the couple who has just been married.

One word about children. Traditionally, having children at a wedding or in a wedding celebration has been considered to be good luck. Include them, if you wish, but remember to assign them duties that are age-appropriate and fit their personalities. An active little girl might hate being a flower girl and standing still throughout the wedding. But she might love talking to people at the wedding book and encouraging them to sign it. Children's attention spans are brief, and they can get restless when they have to sit or stand for long periods. They also always seem to need to eat all of the time. So, if you can, please feed the children as soon as possible.

There is a growing trend in some parts of the country to create children's tables at the reception—one for food and one for child guests. The food suggested is supposedly child appealing: Cheetoes, Goldfish, peanut-butter sandwiches, juice boxes, etc. Personally, I think children's tables are insulting to children and also can brew up more trouble quicker than you can Do a Dew. By seating all of the children at one table removes them from supervisors and protectors (parents). They may not know the other children and feel very uncomfortable. That uncomfortableness sometimes can emerge as bullying or acting out.

Also, any child who comes to a wedding reception with his or her parents is fully capable of enjoying adult food at the regular buffet table or through sit-down fare. It is what they would experience if they went out to a restaurant or to Aunt Gladys's for dinner. Even at very young ages, children can learn good manners and how to behave graciously in a more formal setting. If they can't, then maybe they should make a brief appearance and leave to play video games at home.

And, please, remember that children, like adults, need to preserve their own dignity at any cost. I remember a reception that I worked, where the bride had included all of her day-care children in her wedding party. At the reception, in lieu of tossing the garter and the bouquet, the bride and groom tossed two bears, one dressed as a groom and one dressed as a bride. One little boy was shy and didn't want to go out with the other little boys. The bride and groom got the guests at the reception to coax the little boy to come up and stand with the other boys. When the bear was tossed, the kids scrambled after it like it was the winning football at the Super Bowl. The little boy was mauled and came up crying with a bloody nose. Not only did the incident humiliate and injure the little boy, but totally destroyed the joyous mood at the reception. Make sure that what events you create for children have the children's best interests in mind.

Calendar and Timetable

It's always better to plan as far ahead as you can, especially if the bride and groom live some distance from where they hope to celebrate their wedding. Many brides want to come home to their hometowns to be married, to share their celebration with old friends, and to have the convenience of facilities closer to parents and relatives who might not be able to travel very far. In this instance, it might be helpful to enlist the aid of a wedding consultant/coordinator or a good friend who can help you do the leg work. And don't forget all of the technological conveniences: the internet (for tracking down reception sites, florists, honeymoon destinations, etc.), fax (for sending contracts back and forth), conference calling, etc.

In any case, start planning as soon as possible. It's become common for couples to start planning a year and a half ahead of time. Part of the reason for that is the need to reserve the locations of the ceremony and the reception ahead of time. A popular hall or country club may not be available for the date you want if you don't reserve early and put down the necessary deposits.

Most of the wedding timetables in magazines or on-line suggest starting your planning six to twelve months ahead.

The following timetable captures the entire wedding planning process, including planning the ceremony and the reception.

WEDDING TIME LINE

Nine to Twelve Months

> Select a wedding date and time
> Discuss financial obligations
> Decide on budget
> Decide on style of wedding (type and style)
> Choose location of ceremony
> Choose location of reception
> Choose attendants
> Plan reception
> Select photographer/videographer
> Select florist
> Select caterer
> Select bridal registry
> Discuss honeymoon plans
> Reserve limousine transportation

Six to Nine Months

> Select gown, veil, & accessories
> Select attendants' gowns
> Select men's formalwear
> Select music for ceremony
> Book reception DJ or band
> Compile guest lists (the bride's, the bride's family's, the groom's, the groom's family)
> Order invitations
> Reserve wedding night suite

Four to Six Months

    Finalize honeymoon plans

    Shop for trousseau

    Find a new place to live

    Shop for home furnishings

    Set appointment for a physical exam and update your immunizations if you are going out of the country on your honeymoon

    Set appointments for blood tests (if your state requires them)

    Get passports if you are going out of the country

    Order invitations

    Help mothers select their dresses

    Plan rehearsal dinner (Traditionally, the groom's parents does this.)

    Register for gifts

Two to Four Months

    Purchase wedding rings and have them engraved

    Find out the legal requirements for marriage in your state (when to apply for the license)

    Book accommodations for out-of-town guests

    Book beauty appointments

    Address invitations

    Choose champagne and wines

    Choose reception hall decor

    Choose reception MC

    Check local newspapers about wedding announcement deadline

Reserve rental items necessary for the ceremony or reception

Order wedding and groom's cake

One to Two Months

Mail wedding invitations

Select attendants' gifts

Have a formal portrait taken in wedding gown for newspaper announcement

Purchase gifts for each other

Investigate legal details (changing beneficiaries, consolidating auto insurance, bank accounts)

Decide on a seating plan for the reception

Make arrangements to get foreign money for the honeymoon if you are going out of the country

Be sure attendants are informed of rehearsal plans, gown fittings, etc.

Arrange for final fitting of your gown

Confirm honeymoon trip reservations and check luggage

Test new hairstyles you may be considering

Arrange for ice sculptures for reception

Select reception music

Complete arrangements with photographer, florists, caterer, musicians/singers, DJ/band, reception hall, wedding officiator

Write vows

Send copies of ceremony readings to wedding participants

Two Weeks

Follow up calls for invitations (unless your guests are very polite and they respond to RSVP's)

Record wedding gifts as you receive them and write thank-you notes promptly

Double check wedding attire and accessories for entire wedding party

Confirm time and date of wedding rehearsal with wedding party

Review reception seating plans and prepare place cards if necessary

Arrange to move your belongings to your new home

Select wedding announcements

One Week

Buy traveler's checks for honeymoon

Pack for honeymoon

Have a final consultation with caterer, florist, musicians/singers, DJ/band, MC, photographer/ v i d e o - grapher, officiant, reception hall, wedding ceremony site

Give final guest count to reception facility and caterer

Host bridesmaid's luncheon

Make sure that everyone arriving from out-of-town is met by someone, knows where everyone else is staying, etc.

Budget

Weddings can be very pricey. According to a 1993 arti-cle in Forbes, the average wedding costs $19,000, with first-rate events averaging $50,000. And, of course, we've all heard of celebrity weddings that cost millions. An international model recently spent $35,000 on her wedding gown alone–much of that was for flying in special seamstresses to bead the dress. Entertainment for the wedding reception can cost several thousand dollars, and catering and wedding cakes can also be pricey. When you add in wedding attire and accessories, decorations, gifts for attendants, invitations, etc., the total cost can easily approach that $19,000 average.

Today, parents of the bride don't always foot the bill for the wedding. Diane Warner, a nationally-known wedding consultant, states that 70% of all engaged couples pay for their own weddings. Sometimes, the bride's parents and the groom's parents also contribute.

Setting up your wedding budget may not sound like a fun thing to do since you've been dreaming about your wedding date, but that single act will shape every decision that you'll make from this point on. You may not want to decide on every little penny from the outset but you will need to know what is the financial limit to your choices. If you want to keep costs down, there are several books available to help you plan your wedding on a tight budget. (See resource list.) Most importantly, since you and your fiancé will pay for the wedding, you can feel freer to make your own choices and not feel so obligated to bow to the wishes of your families in areas that you don't want to.

The breakdown of wedding costs* is reflected in the following typical wedding categories:

| Reception | 50% of total cost |
| Bride's dress/accessories | 10% |

Flowers	10%
Music	10%
Photography/videography	10%
Invitations/postage	4%
All other expenses	6%

(*From Diane Warner)

Of course, any of these categories can be adjusted according to your preferences. If you need to spend less in some areas, those might be in the flowers or invitations, or even the wedding gown itself. And, you can always adjust your reception costs, depending on what you are planning. For example, a favorite uncle might belong to an organization which could secure a hall at a discount or a friend might donate his ranch to host an outdoor reception.

Size

There are two very important initial decisions you will need to make regarding your budget. How big do you want the wedding to be? and What kind of wedding?

Size of the wedding is usually determined in general first. Do you want a small, intimate wedding with just your parents and some very close friends? Or, do you want to invite your entire hometown and celebrate for hours? That decision will set the tone for the wedding style you will choose. It also will help shape your budget. A small, intimate wedding and reception naturally will not cost as much as a-pull-out-the-stops wedding reception and dance at a country club.

Size, however, may change once you start comparing your guest lists with your parents' guest lists. Try to only invite people you care about the most and who have been involved with your life. Just remember, though, that each added guest will create additional costs for food and drink and perhaps in extra seating and tables. More guests may also mean that you may need to move the reception to a larger facility.

Wedding Style

Once you determine the size of your wedding and reception, then you are ready to look at your wedding style. Finding your style means looking at the type and theme your want for your wedding.

Type–time of day

There are two concerns when deciding wedding type. The first is the time of day you want to have your wedding and reception. In America today, you can get married at almost any time of day or night on any day of the week. The only constraints are those of availability of the wedding facilities and the officiant, and the flexibility of your guests. It is perfectly OK to have a wedding and reception in the morning, at noon, at tea time, in the evening, or even at midnight.

Some couples choose morning weddings with a breakfast or brunch reception. Sometimes couples want to catch the morning light at a specific place or they want to get married and then catch an early plane to their honeymoon destination. Others just want to start the day married and then be able to carry out a series of festivities throughout the rest of the day. Still others find a brunch less expensive than an evening buffet and dance. Regular breakfast fare is served along with

12

wedding cake and lots of hot coffee and tea. Champagne and champagne punch may also be served.

Luncheon receptions usually follow a wedding at 11:00 or 12:00. The buffet or sit-down meal is served between 12:00 and 2pm. If a hall is rented, the wedding dance can follow, with guests leaving no later than about 4pm. Reception menus for luncheons are very similar to evening receptions, except the portions may be smaller. It is very acceptable to provide champagne at a luncheon reception, and bar service may be provided as well.

A tea or cocktail reception comes after an early afternoon wedding. The tea reception is usually served between 2pm and 5pm. Tea sandwiches and finger foods are served with coffee and tea. A champagne punch may also be served. This is the least expensive reception to provide. You can entertain a large number of guests with a small amount of cash outlay.

The cocktail reception is served later, between 4pm and 7:30pm. Wine, beer, and champagne punch are offered with hot and cold hors d'oeuvres. Bar service also may be provided. You can also provide music for dancing or ambiance here as well as at the tea reception.

The most common reception type is the evening reception with a dinner served either sit-down or as a buffet. This is also the most costly due to the fact that you are providing a complete meal, liquor, and usually a dance band or a DJ for entertainment. Catering, decorating, liquor choices, the wedding cake, and entertainment are the most costly expenditures. These are also areas where you can try to trim costs.

Type–formality

The second question you must decide when determining wedding type is the degree of formality you want at your wedding and reception. It is usually not cool to mix very formal with informal. Though size is usually the first indicator of a formal or informal type of reception, you can have a very large informal gathering and you can have a small, intimate very formal affair.

Very Formal. Usually, these events are very large, serving over 200 people. The location is elegant: a country club, a ballroom, an historic estate, or a museum. The bride is dressed in a traditional gown with a chapel or cathedral length train (shorter during the day). Between 4 and 12 bridesmaids wear floor-length gowns. Groom and groomsmen wear white-tie and tails for an evening wedding or cutaway coats for the daytime. A live band usually plays the wedding dance. Flowers and decorations are elegant. Tables are dressed with fine linens and china, silver, and crystal. Chairs often have slipcovers in the bride's colors or the colors of the wedding theme.

Formal. This type of reception is very similar to the very formal, except it's for a smaller crowd, usually over 100 guests. The reception site can be a church hall, hotel ballroom, club, or home. The bride wears a long gown with a chapel, sweep, or detachable train. She may wear a shorter gown if the wedding is scheduled during the day. Her attendants (2-6) can wear either short or long dresses. The groom and his merry men wear gray strollers, waistcoats, striped trousers and ties for day or black tuxedos for evening. Again, a sit-down reception is usually served, although a formal tea or cocktail reception can be offered. A jazz combo or string quartet can provide ambience, depending on your theme. You can also have a wedding dance.

Semi-formal. Again, similar to formal but a tad more folksy for a group of less than 100 people. The reception location can be either indoors or outdoors, at a beach or park, a private home, hotel, church hall, or banquet facility. The bride can wear whatever length gown she wants in whatever color she wants. She can have a short or long veil. Her attendants (between 1 and 3) can wear whatever they wish also. The groom and groomsmen usually wear suits and ties for a day wedding and tuxedos or dinner jackets for an evening one. A buffet is usually served instead of a sit-down dinner. Music can be either a band or DJ.

Informal. Here the reception is for a small intimate group, usually less than 50 at a home or restaurant. The bride can wear a suit or dress in whatever color she wants. There is usually only one attendant who wears a suit or short dress. The groom and best man wear suits or blazers with slacks. Music can also be a live band or DJ.

These degrees of formality are generalities. There have been quite tasteful weddings that have bent these rules. If you want fewer attendants at your formal wedding, you can do that. If you want more at your very informal wedding, you can do that, too. You can do whatever you want at your wedding as long as your guests are prepared for it.

One other consideration about type is really a reflection on your personality. Are you a traditional person or a non-traditional person? Your wedding can reflect either. The following profiles are examples of the traditional, traditional with flair, and non-traditional personalities.

Traditional personality

You are interested in following what Ms. Manners says.

You plan your wedding according to a classic wedding planner.

You want to be introduced at the reception as Mr. & Mrs.

You want to wear your mother's wedding gown.

You want your reception to be a formal sit-down dinner.

You thought Lady Di's wedding was the model for the perfect wedding.

Traditional with a flair personality

A theme wedding sounds like fun but you want to keep it tasteful.

You want to be introduced as, "The wedding couple: John Smith and Mary Jones-Smith."

You want to write your own vows.

You want to do everything the wedding books say but you want to do it your way.

You'd rather get married in a pastel color or a white dress that fits your theme.

Nontraditional personality

The idea of a big, formal wedding makes you sweat.

You plan a wedding totally out of the ordinary–like a sky-diving wedding or an underwater wedding.

You want to write your own wedding ceremony.

You really want to hire a zydeco band and serve Cajun food.

You don't want to register for gifts; you want the surprise of finding out just how well your friends and family know you.

A barefoot beach wedding is appealing to you.

You want your wedding and reception to be something that your friends and family will talk about for years.

You want to be married in any color except white or ivory.

Your wedding rings will be designed by an artist that you know personally.

You want to be married at Disneyland.

You want to be introduced as, "The wedding couple: John Smith and Mary Jones."

The wedding band is the group you and your fiancé toured with last summer.

Theme

Theme weddings may naturally form out of special circumstances. For example, you or your fiancé are members of the military. It would only be natural to have a military wedding with all of the trimmings reflecting that.

Another natural theme is one of ethnicity. For example, if you are Asian, you might want to be married in red and decorate your reception hall with traditional colors or decorations that reflect your heritage. Almost any ethnic or cultural background could be brought into a wedding theme. There are new wedding books and wedding consultants who specialize in Irish weddings or African-American weddings.

Some couples want to recapture a time long ago, either because they are members of a recreationist group like SCA, the Society for Creative Anachronism, or because they just thought that time period was special. SCA weddings are medieval, courtly weddings with knights and ladies. There is information on the internet and in some publications on just how to create a medieval wedding. They offer authentic advice about wedding attire and even the wedding feast, which, in those times, was a many-course affair that went on for hours. These feasts often are prepared by SCA members who have special skills in catering these affairs, and they are well worth the time to cultivate their acquaintance. The food is definitely worth it.

Some of the more accessible themes that couples have tried have revolved around other time periods. A Big Band wedding would capture the feel of the 1940's. The bride might wear an antique gown or a copy and long over-the-elbow gloves. The reception, of course, would have a full swing orchestra with lots of champagne flowing.

Other time periods could be a Roaring Twenties wedding, a Victorian wedding, a Renaissance wedding, a Southern plantation wedding, or even a Fifties wedding. These aren't silly, over-the-top ideas. They can be pulled off tastefully or with as much impishness as you can muster. Most of these period themes deal with specific types of dress: brocades and velvets for a Renaissance wedding; high-necked lace gowns or wispy, angelic chiffons for a Victorian wedding; hoopskirts and parasols for a Southern plantation wedding; strings of pearls and lace smocking for a Roaring Twenties wedding;

and even full-skirted, pinch-waisted gowns for a Fifties wedding.

Some of these themes would be perfect at specific locations. For instance, a Southern plantation wedding could be held at a park or formal garden or at a museum or turn-of-the-century hall or country club. A Victorian wedding might be great at an historic building, a garden, or a castle.

Other kinds of themes might involve wreaths, candles, hearts, or doves. Some other ideas are holidays (especially if your wedding falls near Christmas) or a season (snowball theme for winter or a beach wedding for summer). Other themes may revolve around your wedding colors. Finally, if you are marrying in the West or in a rural area (or you just like the theme), you might want to do a western wedding or a country wedding, complete with a horse and buggy in lieu of a limousine. Some couples have had the following themes: cruise ship, Oktoberfest, African safari, carousel, or Autumn harvest. Some have even drawn their wedding theme from their honeymoon destination, setting up a Polynesian or rain forest theme.

Finally, one really popular wedding theme is the vacation resort or amusement park theme. These weddings actually take place at a vacation resort or amusement park. Disneyland and Walt Disney World both have wedding planners to create a fairy tale wedding. They provide everything from catering, flowers, makeup artists, photographers, and the perfect wedding cake. You can also ride in Cinderella's Glass Coach for an extra fee.

SeaWorld, Knott's Berry Farm, Busch Gardens, and Opryland all have wedding packages. Knott's Berry Farm even offers art deco decorations and ice sculptures. SeaWorld throws in the flowers and a harpist. You can also have a sea lion act as ring bearer. Busch Gardens presents an elegant wedding with hors d'oeuvres, fine wines and champagnes, dinner, flowers, and entertainment–all at the Crown Colonial House. These theme park weddings provide everything–for a price. Usually, if you only want your parents to witness your wedding, or just your best man and maid of honor, these packages are affordable. They can be cost prohibitive for large weddings, however.

Finally, one other theme type wedding is the honeymoon wedding. There are wedding consultants in exotic places like Bermuda or Jamaica who handle an out-of-the-country wedding. You can legally be married in another country, have the event photographed, enjoy a fine dinner afterwards, and sometimes have a few days at a resort thrown in–all for a flat fee.

Location

Determining your wedding style will help you decide where to hold your wedding ceremony and reception. When these early decisions are made, you can then book a hall, garden, country club, or your Aunt Myrtle's backyard. Whatever you decide, make sure that your location is accessible to all of your guests. If you have elderly relatives or friends in wheelchairs, make sure that the facility will accommodate them. Most public places now must comply with Americans with

Disabilities Act codes, therefore you will have ramps or elevators on site as well as wheelchair accessible bathrooms.

Reception sites vary in price and creativity. Some can be quite inexpensive to rent for the day or evening. Just make sure what is included and not included. For instance, some halls may rent you the space but will not provide tables and chairs, nor the catering. If you rent tables and chairs or even tents, some rental companies may expect you to set them up and break them down afterwards. In addition, some halls will provide the tables and chairs but no table linens, table service, or flatware—or it is an additional cost. Finally, determine who sets up and when and who cleans up. You don't want to spend most of your wedding day setting up your reception or cleaning up afterwards.

Some of the locations for your wedding reception can be religious halls, lodges, clubs, hotels, restaurants, gardens, historic homes, and private homes. Below is a breakdown of these different locations and estimates of cost.

Religious halls

You may choose to hold your reception at a banquet hall in the place of worship where your wedding ceremony takes place. Depending on what you want for your reception, this could be a very low cost site. You will need to find out if you can bring in alcohol (if you want to serve it at your wedding). You will need to determine whether the music you want at your wedding reception is acceptable in the church or synagogue's hall. For example, a chamber orchestra or a harpist might be perfect in any location, but a rock band pounding out

Arrowsmith tunes may not fit a very conservative church clientele. Church and synagogue halls often are set up by church volunteers, unless your caterers will do that for you. Therefore, keeping on the good graces of the church ladies may be to your best advantage. Costs can run $100 and up.

Lodges and halls

Nearly every town has a VFW, American Legion, Knights of Columbus, or Elks Hall. There are many other fraternal and service organizations that offer their facilities to members' families or to the community at large. Like religious halls, you will need to find out what is provided: tables and chairs, set up and clean up. These facilities often have their own bars so a cash bar is always an option. You will need to find out if you can bring in your own champagne or whether you can buy a keg from the facility. Some facilities charge a corking fee when you bring your own champagne. Usually, you can bring in your own caterer, but you will need to check whether your caterer can use their kitchens to hold food until serving. The cost can run from $300 and up.

Clubs, hotels, and restaurants

Many hotels and fine restaurants have separate banquet facilities. Any of these would be good for a sit-down dinner or buffet with or without light music. For a full wedding dance, you may need to determine if the banquet space is big enough or has a separate dance floor. You will need to determine noise restriction for your wedding music. Who determines how loud it is?

These facilities often have full kitchens and caterers at your disposal. They also have the ability to set up a cash bar or otherwise provide beer and wine. You will need to find out whether you can bring in your own caterer if you wish or whether you must order your reception food through the restaurant or hotel. Do they charge an extra fee to pour coffee with the cake? Will they have adequate wait staff on site or will you have to pay for extra help?

Banquet coordinators at hotels and restaurants are very skilled in wedding reception planning and can give you much needed advice. Just remember that they are representing their facility's kitchen and may push to sell their product. If the menu and costs are within your wedding budget and correspond to your wedding style, it may be a great choice.

Costs can range from a few hundred dollars to into the thousands, depending on whether the facility provides catering or not. Some small restaurants can be rented out for an entire evening. Costs can be competitive with a banquet facility that provides catering.

Private homes and gardens

Having your wedding reception at your parent's home may allow you more flexibility and more opportunity to do things your way. However, though the site may be free, costs can start to add up if you are renting tents, tables, linens, etc. You will need to determine whether the location will accommodate all of your guests and whether there is adequate guest parking. You will also need to provide sufficient bathroom facilities for your guests. That may involve renting portable toilets. Additionally, you will need to look at your lighting needs, especially if you are holding your reception outside after dark.

Finally, you will need to notify your neighbors that you will be having a reception on a particular day. In some towns, you will need to get a noise variance for your reception so that your guests' laughter and your wedding music doesn't cause your neighbors to call the police. People often get noise variances for block parties, and since all of the neighbors are invited, there usually isn't a problem.

Costs may be free for the site, but rentals and extra serving or parking help may add up.

Public facilities: Gardens, museums, and historic homes

Public facilities can be quite inexpensive for a wedding ceremony. Call your local Historical Society or Chamber of Commerce for suggestions about historic buildings, private mansions, wineries, or art galleries. City, county, and state facilities are also reception possibilities. These can include state or county parks (some have nice lodges), university or college facilities, castles, museums, libraries, public gardens, and marinas.

Costs can begin to mount as well as complications about permissions to use the facilities when you plan a reception at these sites. Liability reasons are given most often. There is concern about guests' welfare as well as the integrity of the site itself. Having a big wedding dance with a rock band and lots of messy food and drink could put off curators of museums, causing them to worry about the safety of the art displayed or the facility itself. When you are dealing with food and drink, there always is spillage and breakage.

Location Checklist

Always visit the reception site before you decide. Make sure you see the actual room where the reception will be held and ask lots of questions. Here's a checklist for what to look for.

Decor

Is the facility's decoration in keeping with your wedding theme?

Will you need to bring in decorations that fit your theme?

Will those decorations work in the facility?

Size

Will the hall accommodate all of your guests?

Is there a dance floor?

Is there a stage for a band or will one need to be brought in?

Is there ample room to move around the head table and the buffet table?

Is there a place where the DJ can be set up?

Location

How close is the facility from the wedding ceremony site?

Is it easy to find?

Parking, bathrooms, access

Is there enough parking?

Are there enough bathrooms and where are they located?

Is the facility handicap accessible?

Is there adequate power and electrical needs for the band or DJ?

Is there a PA system available? Is there an extra charge for its use?

Is there adequate wait staff? Do you pay extra for the wait staff?

Are extra tables available for the cake, gifts, and guest book?

Permissions

Is alcohol permitted?

Can you bring in your own alcohol?

Can you bring in your own caterer or is one provided?

Is a band or loud music permitted?

Who determines whether the music is too loud?

Will you or your caterer have access to the ice machine, kitchen refrigerator, etc.?

Is this a non-smoking facility?

Can you use rice or confetti?

Can you furnish your own cake?

Can you put decorations on the walls or ceiling?

Set up and clean up

Who sets up?

Who cleans up?

What does clean up entail?

Price

What is the rental fee?

Is the fee based on an hourly rate or for a full night?

What is included—tables, linens, flatware, stemware, china, serving dishes, coffee pots, punch bowls?

Is catering available? Is it included in the fee?

What is not included?

If tables, linens, etc. are not provided, how much will it cost to rent? Who will set these up?

Is bar service available?

Is there a fee if you don't vacate the facility on time?

Does the fee include taxes and gratuities?

Deposit

Is a deposit require?

How much?

When must it be paid?

When do you pay the balance?

Availability

Is the facility available for the date you want?

For how long will you have the facility rented?

What time do they close the doors?

When is last call?

What other events will be taking place at the facility on your wedding day?

CATERING

Choosing a caterer may be as delicate a matter as finalizing the reception menu. You will need to do a bit of research before you start talking with prospective caterers. Find out who catered your friend's or relative's recent wedding. Go to receptions and taste the food. Research who knows how to make your favorite dish for 200 people. Your reception facility might take care of your catering needs or make recommendations of local caterers that they have worked with.

When you have a list of potential caterers, get on the phone and make appointments to talk with them about their services. Find out what kind of insurance they have, how long they have been in business, and what kind of references they have. Make sure they will still be in business when your wedding comes around. Check their credentials with the Better Business Bureau. Does the caterer have a catering license or a recent business license? Ask to see her current Board of Health permit. Caterers with licenses and permits must adhere to strict health codes. Don't risk food poisoning on someone's recommendation alone.

Every caterer should keep a scrapbook to show off dish presentation and table display. Look at pictures of recent events they've catered to see how the dishes look and how professional the catering staff looks.

Make sure that you choose a caterer who can provide the menu that you want. Don't ask for quiche from the kitchens of your favorite ribs house. Has the caterer served many receptions for the number of people on your guest list? How big are the portions? Can the caterer provide alternatives for guests with special dietary needs? For instance, can the caterer provide a kosher or vegetarian selection, clearly labeled, on the buffet table or provide either as a special meal for a sit-down dinner? Does the caterer prepare all of the food with her own staff or does she subcontract it out?

Determine what details the caterer can provide. Some caterers only provide the food. Others include table set up and decorations, liquor, cake, equipment rentals, and wait service. Who will be on site the day of your wedding? Who will supervise the reception? How many servers will be on hand? Will the caterer provide a bartender or extra busers? Will the caterer provide clean up and recycling?

Try to arrange a taste session. Perhaps you could sample an hors d'oeuvre tray from a recent reception or samples of the main dishes.

Fees are usually set by a price per person. When you first meet with the caterer, you will be using a rough estimate of the number of guests you will have. The final count will come a couple of weeks before the wedding when all of your RSVP's have been recorded. Service charges and sales tax can add as much as 15% to 20% on top of the bill. You may be required to put down a deposit from 50% to 70% of the final cost.

Make sure you receive a complete contract, detailing all of the services that the caterer will provide. The contract should specify the following items:

$ Date, time, and location of your wedding reception. Please include the hours that the catering service will be provided.

$ Date when the final head count must be given to the caterer.

$ List of services that the caterer will provide in complete detail (the type of meal–buffet or sit-down dinner-liquor, cake, table service and serving pieces, ice, wait staff, decorations, ice sculpture, flowers, etc.).

$ The complete menu, including hors d'oeuvres, liquor, and set ups.

$ Fees, including all additional charges (cork fees, cake cutting, taxes, gratuities, overtime, etc.), payment schedule, and when the final balance is due.

$ The name of the supervisor or manager who will be handling your wedding reception on site.

$ The change policy of the caterer as well as the cancellation policy.

$ The refund policy, if you are unhappy.

Tell the caterer up front what you are willing to spend for an estimated number of guests. Get several estimates. See what the caterer will negotiate. Perhaps the caterer will provide a more expensive entree or wine instead of a discount in the fee.

Food

The first consideration when talking menu with your caterer is your wedding style and time of day for your reception. If you cannot afford a full dinner, there are other options that may fit your wedding style and the time of day of your wedding.

A simple cake and punch reception can be held any time—mid morning, mid afternoon, or late evening. Just be sure not to schedule it right at a meal time. You can also add nuts, mints, and special cookies to the cake table. Make sure that you note on your invitations that a cake and punch reception will follow the ceremony. Your guests will not expect a meal then.

Other simple receptions are the tea reception, the salad reception, the hors d'oeuvres reception, and the dessert reception. Tea receptions are usually held between 2 pm and 4 pm and usually consist of dainty, tea sandwiches, coffee, tea, and punch. Salad receptions can be held mid morning or early afternoon. At them, serve a variety of salads–green salads, pasta salads, potato salads, rice or Chinese salads, fruit, and gelatins. A desert reception can be held between 1 pm and 4 pm. You can serve pies, cookies, brownies, pastries, or even sundaes, in addition to wedding cake. Any of these receptions should be noted on the invitations.

The hors d'oeuvres reception can be held any time from 11:00 am to 5 pm. If you serve cocktails, then the hors d'oeuvres reception should be held between 5 pm and 7 pm. If you serve seafood or meat hors d'oeuvres (oysters on the half shell, shrimp cocktail, cocktail sausages, or chicken wings), you should note on the invitations that an hors d'oeuvres reception will follow the ceremony. If you don't serve seafood or meat, you call it a light hors d'oeuvres reception. Light hors d'oeuvres can be cheese trays, vegetable platters, fruit platters, and chips and dips.

Buffets and sit-down meals are acceptable for wedding brunches, early afternoon weddings, and evening receptions.

Costs for buffet or sit-down can be similar. Sometimes there is less waste at a sit-down dinner, since a complete plate is served to each guest. However, if you are unsure of the exact number of guests that you'll have (as in the case of the wedding dance where the whole town is invited or is open to more than the wedding ceremony guests), you may find the buffet quite adequate and very economical.

Menu choices for buffets and sit-down dinners can vary. Whatever you decide, make sure that you select foods with your guests' tastes in mind. Don't serve quail under glass for your family and friends who enjoy hot wings or lasagna. Also, be sensitive to special dietary needs of your guests. It doesn't cost very much to add a handful of special meals (for example, kosher, vegetarian, no milk) to a sit-down affair. It can get a bit costly if you offer equal choices on your buffet table, however. But you can add a platter of veggie pasta or a cheese tray to the buffet table at little extra cost, if you are expecting your cousin's vegetarian friends.

Morning brunch menus can offer pastries, a variety of fruits, omelets, juice, and coffee and tea. You can also offer champagne cocktails and Bloody Mary's if you wish. Some couples choose to have a do-it-yourself waffle bar. You can supplement all of this with sausages and bacon. Most of these foods can be kept warm and quite tasty on a steam table.

The luncheon or dinner buffet or sit-down menu can vary with your own personal tastes. You can serve everything from cold cuts to hot entrees. Wines and champagne can also be served, as well as beer. The only limit is your imagination and your budget, and maybe the messiness of the food. You might want to rethink serving ribs or spaghetti because of the potential for dry-cleaning woes on those rented tuxes or even the satin of your wedding gown.

Buffets and sit-down dinners have several different serving options available. Each option has its own merits and expense.

$ Buffets usually have very few servers involved. Mainly, these are people who set up the food and keep the dishes filled and fresh-looking. Sometimes there is extra staff who serve from steam tables or who carve meat. You can cut down on long buffet lines by offering two buffet tables stationed at opposite ends of the hall.

$ One variation on the buffet is the food station. These are areas around the room where your guests can mingle and graze at the same time. You can provide a veritable food journey by having your guests watch someone carve a roast, serve stir fry made before your eyes, or offer you a topping-rich sundae made to your specification. You can add a cheese and bread table, a fresh fruit table, and a finger food table to round out your meal. Food stations can provide an exotic experience for your reception, can cut down on the time guests wait for food, and eliminate the need for a lot of wait staff.

$ American service is most often offered with a typical sit-down dinner. Here, individual plates are dished out and served to each guest. This usually involves hiring a team of servers to produce the food in the most efficient time possible, without too many people having to wait for a plate. This also allows special dietary meals to be served to the correct individuals (especially if you have seated your guests by place cards).

$ Another serving method, especially for smaller receptions, is family style. Here serving dishes are placed at each table and the guests help themselves. This involves fewer servers and usually shortens the time your guests have to wait for something to eat.

$ Finally, Russian service is available in some areas. Like family style, large serving platters are brought to each table, but the food is served by the wait staff, rather like dinner served in an English manor estate. A large number of servers is necessary for this and it can take a lot of time to get food to people. Like family service, this style is best used for smaller receptions.

$ French service involves carving meat and preparing the food at the table. Then platters of food are offered to the guests and they serve themselves. This can be as labor-driven as Russian service because of the need to have experienced cooks carving and preparing the meal.

Costs for either a buffet or sit-down dinner though, can vary. If you get carried away, a buffet can cost more than an elaborate sit-down affair, especially if you are favoring a lot of fancy hor d'oeuvres. These finger foods are labor-intensive because each one is often a work of art. They look wonderful, but will Uncle Harry really care when he stuffs three of them into his mouth at once and then wants to know when the real meal is going to start.

Drink

If you are providing food, you must have something to drink. It can simply be coffee or tea, soft drinks or punch, or fruit juices. If your religious beliefs or preferences do not encourage alcohol consumption, you do not have to provide alcohol at your wedding reception. You can often get around the social pressures of alcohol by planning your wedding reception for a morning breakfast or brunch or an afternoon tea. You can also choose not to provide alcohol at any other type of reception. Choosing not to serve alcohol can also save you lots of money. If your friends and family expect liquor, they will need to go for a cocktail after your reception. This is your day and you can plan whatever you want.

If you have alcohol available, you can save money on your bar bill in a number of ways. First, you can have the hotel or hall provide a cash bar. Guests order what they want and pay for it. Your liquor costs might only be for a few bottles of champagne for the toasts. Some couples go so far as to have guests raise whatever glass is at hand for the toast and share the toast that way. If you are serving wine with dinner, however, you can instruct the wait staff to fill glasses halfway and not to pour at an empty seat.

Try to assure that you can return all unopened bottles of alcohol for credit after the reception. You might also want to tell the caterer or the hotel that you will have someone count empty bottles to ensure an accurate count of alcohol served. I wouldn't use this tactic on the hometown caterer or hotel unless you know that good ole Bob pads his liquor bills. You don't want to antagonize the people in the town you see every day. Otherwise, you'll get a reputation for being stingy. If you still want to keep them honest, you can have someone count the empties and use it as a reference for the bill when you settle up.

A recent poll of alcohol consumers found that 50% of them order beer most often, 35% order hard liquor, and 15% order wine. Some couples choose to serve only beer, wine, and soft drinks at their receptions, with no cash bar available. That's fine if that's what your friends and family drink. You can eliminate wine all together if you have a beer-drinking crowd or vice versa.

As far as estimates of the amount of alcohol to order, you might consider two factors. One is a general rule about ordering.

For beer, order 60% lagers, 30% ales, and 10% lite beers. With today's weight-consciousness, you might want to order more lite beers. If you have a family who enjoys hardy ales, then order more of them.

For wine, order 60% white and 40% red. Medium dry wines are the most popular, though you might want to offer a sweeter wine with the cake.

The other technique is to determine how many servings for each size bottle.

Bottle	Milliliters	Ounces	Ounces per glass	Glasses per bottle
Wine/spirits	750	26.4	4 or 1 ½	6 to 7
Wine	1000	35.2	4	8
Spirits	1140	40.13	1 ½	26
Wine	1500	52.8	4	13
Spirits	1750	61.6	1 ½	41
Wine	4000	140.8	4	35

If you are ordering beer by the keg, remember that domestic beer kegs are sized differently from imported kegs. For domestic beer, a half-barrel keg contains 15.5 gallons and a quarter-barrel keg contains 7.75 gallons. Using a 10-ounce plastic cup, you can get less than 200 cups out of the half-barrel and about 100 cups from a quarter-barrel. Imported kegs contain about 10.7 gallons per half-barrel. Be careful because some domestic taps will not fit an imported keg.

Cake

History

Cakes have been part of wedding celebrations since communities met and wished fertility onto a newly married couple. The ancient Greeks baked honey and sesame flour cakes dipped in wine, bacchyllis. The Romans made a cake from wheat flour, salt, and water that was more like bread. It was called a confarreatio and burned over an open flame. It signified that a legal marriage had taken place and that the woman was now under the protection of her husband.

Wheat and other grain cakes in other communities were broken over the bride's head to ensure that she would have many children. Her cake had to be made for her and given as a gift, otherwise she would not have good luck. It was said to be very auspicious if guests caught some of the cake crumbs.

In medieval times, every guest was supposed to bring a cake, and all of them were stacked up. In Shakespearean England, wheat cakes were carried to the church by the bridesmaids and were blessed by the priest. They were then eaten by the bride and groom after the ceremony. It wasn't until

Elizabethan times that a French chef decided to frost the stack of cakes with white sugar frosting so that they would be all of a piece.

The cake of Elizabethan and Victorian England began to take on more and more embellishments. The fruits, nuts, and spices were added to the little wheat cakes, and they were stacked with applesauce between the layers. When processed sugar was developed in Europe and America, wedding cakes were decorated with more flair. Almond marzipan and white sugar icing covered the fruitcakes. Some of the sugar decorations resembled flowers, fans, and lace. Often little charms were baked into the cake for good luck. It wasn't until the Civil War that white, vanilla wedding cakes began to be baked.

The wedding couple used to send guests home with slices of cake all boxed up. It was especially important to send cake to those you couldn't come to the wedding. It is a custom that has sadly gone out of fashion.

Today, the bride and groom share a bit of cake to symbolize the life they are sharing together. Having both the groom and bride cut the cake came about out of necessity. As the wedding cake grew more elaborate, it was difficult for the bride to cut through all of those layers of cake. She needed her husband's strength to do it.

Types of cakes

As you talk with friends and look through bridal magazines, you will find that you can have practically any kind of flavor wedding cake you want and have it decorated any way you want. For years, it was customary to have a multilayered cake, separated by pillars, fountains, and dowels. In the early eighties after Lady Diana's wedding, hexagonal cakes were popular. Today, the trend is a stacked cake without pillars. The cake layers can be round, hexagonal, or square.

To save money, some couples are opting for a small wedding cake and then serving their guests from large sheet cakes. Some caterers will spirit the wedding cake off to the kitchen after the bride and groom have their cake cutting photos taken. The staff will then serve the guests from sheet cakes and box up the wedding cake for the couple to put in their freezer to eat on their first wedding anniversary. Still other couples who really want to go cheap can assemble a dummy wedding cake (much like the displays in bakeries) and serve the guests from sheet cakes in the kitchen.

In some parts of the United States, it is customary to serve a groom's cake as well as a wedding cake. These are usually small, rich cakes. Some have been traditionally chocolate; others have been little spice cakes or fruitcakes. They are served in thin slices beside the wedding cake.

Flavors and decorations

Wedding cake flavors have surpassed the common vanilla with lemon or vanilla custard filling. You can get German chocolate, chocolate mouse, or plain chocolate–and even carrot cake.

You can even have orange, rum, apple, strawberry, raspberry, or spice filling. Try to avoid seed or coconut fillings. All of it can be topped with marzipan, fondant, buttercream, whipped cream, pulled sugar, spun sugar, pastillage, or gold or silver leaf.

Confused? Well, here's a quick glossary of bakery terms.

Buttercream. A sugar icing made with butter and flavored with liqueurs and other flavorings (including vanilla). It can be colored almost any shade and is used to create decorative borders and rosettes. It can also be used as a filling. It is sensitive to heat and humidity and may melt under those conditions, which is a special consideration for outdoor wedding receptions.

Fondant. Another sugar icing made with the addition of corn syrup and gelatin. It is rolled out with a rolling pin and draped over the cake. It serves as a canvas for gum paste flowers and architectural designs. It has a porcelain look and should not be refrigerated.

Ganache. Made from chocolate and heavy cream, it is thicker than mousse but lighter than fudge. It is used for icing or filling. Like buttercream, it will soften in humid weather.

Gum paste. A mixture of sugar, cornstarch, and gelatin, it can be used to mold edible fruits and flowers. They can be kept for years as keepsakes. They don't taste as good as marzipan.

Marzipan. This is made from ground almonds, sugar, and egg whites. It is molded into edible flowers, fruit, and figures. It can also be rolled and used like fondant.

Pastillage. This is a sugary dough that dries hard and is used to mold flowers.

Pipping. Icing dispensed through a pastry bag. It is used to create decorative details like leaves, borders, basketweave patterns, and flowers.

Pulled sugar. Melted sugar syrup that is pulled into flowers, ribbons, and bows.

Royal icing. This icing is made of egg whites, confectionary sugar, and lemon juice. It is piped to create flowers, beads, bows, latticework, and basketweave designs.

Silver and gold leaf. Edible real gold and silver icing used as accents on flowers or lace.

Spun sugar. Caramelized sugar is dropped so that strands form, creating a golden veil over cakes. It is highly vulnerable to humidity. Cakes with spun sugar cannot be displayed for very long before the sugar melts.

Whipped cream. This is your typical whipped heavy cream which is used as an icing or a filling. It must be kept refrigerated and is not suitable for an outdoor wedding.

Some couples are opting for decorate their wedding cakes with silk or cut flowers. If you use edible flowers like nasturtiums, squash blossoms, or pansies, make sure that they have been thoroughly washed. Better yet, get them from a local organic gardener. If you use flowers from your florist, remember that the flowers may have been sprayed with herbicides in the fields and may even have been treated with preservatives. Try to rinse them before you put them on the cake or only use them on top of the cake in place of a cake topper and line the cake with parchment paper for health safety.

Many bride's are choosing not to put a cake topper on the wedding cake itself. Years ago, every wedding cake had a little plastic bride and groom on top. They were replaced with doves and wedding bells. Over the years, these cake toppers have become more elaborate and often weigh so much that they can crash through a cake layer. Today, many brides display a beautiful porcelain cake topper on the cake table but do not put it on the cake. Some dispense with the cake topper all together.

Also, there is a trend to decorate wedding cakes in colors other than varying shades of white or cream. The bride's colors are often reproduced. Other cakes are frosted in pale pastels. If you ask your baker to match your wedding gown or other fabric colors, bring a 3-inch square swatch. Dark colors are hardest to match, with red the most difficult.

One final note about frostings. There is a so-called low-calorie frosting that a number of commercial bakeries are using. Some call it Bettercream because it doesn't use butter or margarine and comes in vanilla and chocolate—or at least white and brown icing. It has no flavor and tastes an awful lot like whipped shortening. If you aren't an icing connoisseur, it just might be your cup of tea. But for any real cake eater, get real buttercream. Your guests will thank you.

Tips

There are a couple of things to remember when you order your cake. Find out if the baker will assemble the cake on site. This is usually the best plan. However, the cake will need to be set up and ready before the reception. The cake will need to sit at room temperature for about three to four hours before it can be cut and served. And, please try not to move the cake once it is set up. Your caterers can move the cake to the kitchen for cutting if it has been placed on a rolling cart or other wheeled table.

If you use gum paste flowers on your cake, remember that they are made on wires or toothpicks. Whoever cuts your cake, will need to remove them before cutting slices. Also, remove strings of artificial pearls that you have used for decoration from your cake before slicing.

Bakers

If, however, you want to invest in your wedding cake as the showpiece of your reception, then find the best baker that you can. There are many options: commercial bakeries, caterers, and specialty bakers.

You can find any commercial bakery to do your cake. They are experienced and offer a variety of styles. Costs are usually reasonable for cakes. Bakeries however may not be as flexible as you'd like. For example, maybe you want German chocolate cake or carrot cake for your wedding cake. Many commercial bakeries aren't equipped to bake unusual flavors on a large scale. They use standard commercial mixes and may not have access to these flavors in quantity. For standard flavors and regular wedding decorations, these may be ideal for what you want.

Your caterer may include a wedding cake in your package. The cakes may be wonderful, but you will have to realize that wedding cakes may not be their specialty. They may have limited designs available. Also, you will need to find out if your caterer charges an extra fee to cut your wedding cake, especially if it comes from an outside source.

For the unique wedding cake, you might want to seek out a specialty cake baker. These are people who bake out of their own homes, or through subcontracts with a bakery. They are veritable artists. These folks are hard to find and only through word-of-mouth. You will need to see photographs of their handiwork and have samples to taste.

Linda Golsheft, who is a master cake designer in California, creates true edible works of art. She is able to wrap and drape chocolate or fondant around cakes to copy the fabric of the bride's gown. She adds pearls and sugar paste flowers that can make the wedding cake almost outshine the bride.

You can sometimes order a cake from a fantastic specialty baker and have it flown in for your wedding. Federal Express (800-463-3339) and Delta Dash (a shipping division of Delta Airlines–800-638-7333) can fly in your cake, packed in dry ice, one tier to a box. It will cost you a hefty $300 to ship a 60-pound cake. But shipping is not without its mishaps. If you decide to ship in a cake, make sure that you secure the services of a local baker to reconstruct the cake once it arrives and fix anything that might have happened to it.

You might try to ferret out other unusual cake bakers. There might be someone who caters museum or gallery openings who happens to bake incredible desserts. I know a bride who went to a local heath food restaurant and asked the cook if he could bake a wedding cake from their terrific carrot cake recipe. He experimented with quantity and created a beautiful three-tiered cake, complete with cream cheese roses.

Other brides have had their aunts or friends make their wedding cake as a gift to the couple. It's a lot to ask of a friend or relative, but if the person is an excellent baker and wants to give such a gift, it might be the perfect choice. It would be very appropriate for a small wedding or for the wedding cake the bride and groom cut. It is often more difficult to bake large sheet cakes in home ovens because they are not as big as commercial ovens.

Contract details

When you have selected a few bakers who might be able to bake the kind of wedding cake you want, set up an interview with each. Try to schedule it early in the week because they will probably be very busy getting out orders for the weekend later in the week. Ask lots of questions and try to sample the kinds of cakes the bakers' make.

Cakes are usually ordered on a per slice basis. If you order a smaller wedding cake and supplement with a sheet cake, order the wedding cake for only half the number of guests.

Make sure you have a contract that includes everything that you want on your cake, the size, and the location of the reception.

*　*　*　*　*　*　*　*　*　*　*　*　*

CAKE CHECKLIST

Questions to ask
- How long have you been in business?
- Tell me about the wedding cakes you've made before? What was the most challenging? The easiest?
- May I see pictures of the cakes?
- What is your cost per slice?
- What size cake will serve how many?
- What shape of cakes do you make?
- Do you also make sheet cakes?
- Do you charge extra for special icings like spun sugar?
- What kinds of flavors of cakes do you make? Can you make_____?
- What kinds of fillings do you offer? Can you make _____?
- What kinds of icings do you make? Can you make _____?
- What kinds of decorations can you provide—fondant, flowers, marzipan, live flowers, etc.?
- What kinds of cake toppers do you recommend?
- Is the cake knife included?
- Will you set up the cake?
- When will you need to get into the hall to set up?
- Will you be cutting the cake? Do you charge a fee?
- Do you make groom's cakes?
- What kind do you make?
- How do you decorate them?

- Are there any other costs?
- Do you have a change or cancellation policy?
- What is your deposit?
- When do you need it?
- When do you want the final payment?

Seating

There usually isn't any special seating at a tea, brunch, hors d'oeuvre, or buffet reception. A sit-down dinner may require place cards, especially if there are several specialty meals planned. Your servers will need to know who they are.

The only special tables may be for the wedding party. After all, everyone came to see the bride and groom and will want to see the couple together enjoying their wedding day. Some bridal tables include the bridal couple and their parents. This is especially appropriate for a small, intimate wedding. You may also include the best man and maid of honor here, too. Some bridal tables have the bridal couple and all of the attendants, usually without their dates. A separate table or tables are set up for the parents.

Standard seating arrangements for the bridal table are bridal couple in the center, maid of honor at the groom's left, best man at the bride's right. The other attendants are seated on each side, alternating men and women.

Some people want to also include a special children's table, sometimes with a buffet of their own. As I have said previously, children who come to weddings are perfectly capable of eating the reception foods that the adults are eating. You also may be courting disaster if you seat all of the children together, without adult supervision. Not only are there choking concerns involved, but spillage and mess.

And, you also may have children picking on other children or who might behave badly under stress. I remember at one event, a mother had a very energetic little girl who was about two. She had been over stimulated by the day's events. When she found her cousin, also two years old, in the center of the room, the mother immediately jumped up to rescue her daughter before she pushed her niece down onto the floor. Everyone thought it was wonderful that the two little ones had discovered each other and were hugging. By the time the mother had reached her child, her daughter had bitten the other child on the cheek. Everyone was visibly upset. All of this could have been avoided if the mother had kept her child close to her and met the child's needs.

Teenagers, on the other hand, can be seated together at their own table. The risks of social *faux pas* or injury would be minimal.

At a sit-down dinner, the bridal couple is served first in this order: bride, groom, maid of honor, other attendants, parents, and other guests. When all have been served, the best man presents the traditional toast to the bridal couple.

Gratuities

It is customary, though voluntary, to tip those who help bring all of the elements of a wedding reception together. There are some folks, though, who should not be tipped. You don't need to tip the florist, cake baker, or reception servers directly. Make sure that any gratuities are not in your contract first, then apply a standard formula for the caterer, banquet manager, etc.

Please tip anyone who has gone out of his or her way to make your guests feel welcome and comfortable. For example, a waitress who warmed a bottle for a baby or found applesauce for a fussy child.

Gratuities should be placed in envelopes with each individual's name or title on the front. The wedding coordinator or the wedding hosts should distribute the envelopes. If the wedding hosts are not either the bride's family or the groom's but the bridal couple themselves, assign someone, usually the best man, to take care of that detail for you. You don't want to fuss over details like that on your special day.

Here's a simple breakdown for who to tip and how much.

$ Delivery persons (those who deliver flowers or the cake, etc.)$5-10 each when they deliver.

$ Ceremony or reception musicians $10-20 per person (Optional) depending on the size of the band/orchestra and how long they played.

$ Parking attendants/valets. $0.50 to $1 per car. This should be paid at the end of the evening through the valets' supervisor. Make sure you post a sign that says that tipping has been taken care of by the wedding hosts.

$ Maitre d', banquet manager, caterer. $1 to $5 per guest or 15-20% of the food and drink bill, paid at the end of the reception. If there is more than one person in charge, divide the tip between them. They will tip the wait staff under them.

$ Bartenders 10% of the total liquor bill, paid to the head bartender for him to distribute or divide it among the number of bartenders present.

$ Restroom or coatroom attendants. $0.50 to $1 per guest, paid to the management of the facility. Please post a sign stating that the tip has been paid by the wedding hosts.

CATERING CHECKLIST

Questions to ask
- How long have you been a caterer?
- What is your experience, background, and education?
- Have you handled events of the size and type I am planning?
- Do you have a current catering license, business license, and/or health permit?
- Do you have a liquor license? Do you need one for providing alcohol at the facility of my choosing?
- Are you insured?
- Do yo provide a taste or sample of your menu(s)?
- Do you set up?
- What time do you set up?
- What are your hours of service–for my reception?
- What equipment do you provide?
- What will I have to provide or rent?
- What is the size of the wait staff that will be serving the day of my reception?
- Who will be in charge the day of my reception?
- How will your staff be dressed?

- Is there a fee for buffet or food station servers?
- Do you provide bartenders? Is there an extra charge for them?
- Do you supply the alcohol?
- Do you supply water, ice, set ups, soft drinks, etc.?
- Is there a corking fee if we provide the alcohol?
- Do you provide the cake?
- Do you offer a cake cutting service? Is there an extra charge for it?
- Do you provide champagne for toasting? Is there an extra charge for this?
- When do you need the final head count? Does this include wedding professions (DJ, band, MC, photographers)
- Do you offer anything special discounts for children?
- How much is the deposit? When is it required?
- When is the final payment due?
- Can I make partial payments?
- Are taxes and gratuity included in the fees?
- Is there an overtime charge and when is it enacted?
- What are the costs for alcohol and beverages (coffee, tea, punch)?
- What is the meal charge per person or per dish?
- Do you cleanup? Is there a fee for that?
- Do you provide linens, tables, chairs, china, glassware, tableware, serving dishes and utensils, chair covers?
- Are these items included or are they an extra fee?
- Where do you obtain your rentals?
- Do you subcontract any portion of the catering plan? To whom?
- What is your refund/cancellation policy?

- When is the last date I can change my headcount, menu, or liquor order?
- What is your leftover policy?
- Do you provide a written contract and a guarantee?
- What are your menu choices?
- Is there a kitchen facility available for holding food items or preparation on site? (This applies to an in-house caterer.)
- What is the general time hors d'oeuvres are served? When will the meal be served?
- If you are planning a buffet, will the food be displayed or served to guests?
- What are the size of meal portions?

* * * * * * * * * * * * *

As is typical with planning weddings, things change. Seeing that I help people plan hundreds of receptions a year, I have to deal with changes all the time. Mostly, brides want to change the time of the reception or the wedding music. Once in awhile, I'll have a bride change her reception location. due to needing a bigger facility or better catering offered. Usually, these are minor changes that are easily remedied. However, one time I think I experienced the change of all changes.

A bride called me and said, "Bill, I have a small change to make in my reception format."

Since I'm pretty flexible, I said as always, "That's no problem. What is it—a change in the time or a song selection?"

"No," she answered matter-of-factly, "the groom's name."

I couldn't believe it. Here we were six months from the wedding, and the bride decides to marry the best man instead! I guess she just wanted to make sure the wedding was perfect!

*   *   *   *   *   *   *   *   *   *   *   *   *

MUSIC AND ENTERTAINMENT

There are many decisions that must be made concerning the entertainment for your wedding reception. When you think of entertainment, most folks think of bands, wedding singers, or disc jockeys. Music is often very much a part of our daily lives and therefore an integral part of our special celebrations. We listen to music at work and in the car. We listen to music to relax us and to energize us. And music also helps create a party mood. Therefore, making decisions about music for a wedding reception is vital to creating the mood that want for your wedding. It is important to remember your wedding style and theme when finalizing your plans.

The Wedding MC

There is one decision that probably should be made before you start selecting your musical choices for the first dance. In order to help everything move along smoothly, you will need to hire or designate a master of ceremonies (MC) for your reception. A wedding MC is responsible for presenting your wedding reception as a packaged piece of entertainment. It doesn't matter whether it is a small, intimate midnight cake and coffee event or a formal sit-down dinner for 300 guests with dancing to a full orchestra. A wedding MC will keep everything flowing and will make sure that all of the traditions of a wedding reception are covered.

There are several things to consider when you go looking for a wedding MC. Most often, a band spokesperson may not have the experience or poise for the job. Consider the likes of a Mick Jagger introducing the bride's 90-year-old grand-mother. It might sound like a good idea (and be a highlight of the wedding for some) but do you think that's the memory you want everyone to take away from your wedding?

Many band leaders, especially local groups (and it doesn't matter if they are rock bands, swing bands, country groups, or polka bands), may not have the poise to speak in front of a crowd. They play music, may sing, and may be able to introduce the band. There are excellent exceptions and please use them if you find such gems in your hometown.

Some wedding DJ's may not have public speaking experience either, especially if you hire the same guy who spins tunes for the local high school dances. Radio station DJ's may not always have social skills either. I've been a wedding DJ for eleven years, and I've been handling wedding MC duties. I, however, have a degree in Speech and am a member of Toastmasters. Also, eleven years of doing wedding MC duties has kept me on my toes and sensitive to what the bridal couple wants.

One other consideration in choosing a wedding MC are professional entertainers and family and friends. You can also run into problems with stand-up comics or professional speakers. Sometimes, they want to be in the spotlight, not the wedding couple. And that's the whole point of having a wedding MC–to make sure the spotlight turns to the bridal couple and those closest to them.

Hiring family and friends can be problematic, if they don't feel poised in front of a crowd or really push the envelope of propriety. In some situations, the best man assumes this duty and runs the whole show. It's a big burden to place on your best man when he already has to run around and take care of toasts, tipping, and last minute details. However, it can work quite nicely for a best man if it is a small wedding reception or he's very organized and speaks well.

The wedding MC should be chosen early and should meet with the couple as soon as possible in order to find out the details of the reception and the order of events. He or she should be open and warm and have a sense of humor, but not necessarily be Eddie Murphy. The MC should write down the bride and groom's names and the names of other special guests and get correct pronunciations. He or she should place limitations on jokes or pranks and make sure nothing gets out of hand. The MC should collect humorous or warm stories about the bridal couple and either tell them or arrange for guests to share those stories briefly. The MC should be able to read cold in order to read telegrams and greetings from family and friends who could not be present for the wedding.

Many of the tasks that the wedding MC does involve introductions. The MC introduces the bridal party, the family, and any special guests. The MC invites guests to serve themselves at the buffet table or announces that the meal is being served. The MC also introduces the dedication dances–the first dance, parents' dance, last dance, and any special honor dance. The MC also announces any unusual wedding customs–the dollar dance or the presentation of a special gift. The MC also sets the stage for the cake cutting, the bouquet toss, and the garter toss. Finally, the MC can keep the dance floor full by coaxing everyone to dance or participate in a special dance, though the DJ or band leader may be able to do this by announcing the Chicken Dance or a Conga line.

Whoever you hire, remember that this is your day, not the entertainer's gig.

* * * * * * * * * * * *

I was working a wedding once when the bride got terribly sick in between the wedding and the reception. The bride and some of her wedding party were out in the foyer of the country club, with the bride stretched out on a bench. The bridesmaids asked, "Bill, what should we do?"

I said to the bride, "You know, if you are really that sick, maybe you need to go to the hospital."

In the meantime, there were about 300 hungry people inside the banquet hall, and the food was ready. When food is ready, it needs to be served. I went up to the microphone and said, very calmly, "Ladies and gentlemen, the bride and groom are out in the foyer area. The bride's just feeling a little bit queasy right now, and she's going to get some air. Meanwhile, we'll just start the dinner by serving the wedding party and the parents first."

At about that time, a fire truck pulled up, lights flashing through the country club windows, making red and blue patterns on the walls. Outside this bank of windows where everyone could see were the rescue squad people rolling in a gurney. A few seconds later, the gurney returned, with the bride on it, her white wedding dress billowing in the breeze, as they rushed her out and put her in the truck. Everybody was looking at me, as if they were saying, "Yeah, right, she needs some air. A tank of oxygen is what she needs."

* * * * * * * * * * * * *

Band or DJ?

There are four main issues to think about when deciding on hiring a live band or orchestra or a wedding DJ. They are ambiance, venue limitations, musical taste, and budget. All of these considerations may be intertwined or distinct in your planning.

Ambiance. Ambiance is tied in with your wedding style and theme. If you are planning an island theme or Cajun wedding reception, you will probably want a live Cajun band, a reggae band, or maybe a steel drum group. If you are planning an elegant tea reception, a harpist or a small chamber orchestra might be ideal. A big band or roaring twenties theme might necessitate hiring a swing band or dance orchestra of some kind. You could hire a wedding DJ to play big band tunes, but it might not have the feel that you had originally planned. If your choices run more toward country, rock, or pop music, and you want your guests to be able to dance all night, then deciding on either a DJ or a live band will take some more thought.

Venue limitations. That brings us to venue limitations. Just how big is the stage area and dance floor at the reception venue? Are the banquet caterer or maitre d' suddenly squawking about limiting the number of band members you can hire and the size of the amplifiers? Venues cannot tell you what size band to hire or how much equipment they can bring. They can tell you that they have space restrictions and noise ordinances. Find out what they are before you sign the contract to rent the hall.

Some six-piece bands can fit onto a four-piece stage area just by how they work out their sound plot. Note also that a three-piece band usually cannot do the job of providing dance music for an entire evening, no matter what the configuration of the band is. Most bands need four people to handle a variety of music–keyboards, bass, drums, and one guitar or bass, drums, guitar, and saxophone. Some three-piece bands (bass, drums, guitar) can work if the music they play is of a special genre and is exactly the kind of music your group wants to dance to or listen to. Slightly larger bands can handle a variety of musical styles and can play slow tunes, fast ones, and the occasional Chicken Dance.

A DJ will almost always fit into a smaller space at the reception hall. Even if the DJ brings concert-size speakers, a DJ and his equipment can be put in an area that won't intrude into the dance floor or interfere with the flow of serving or mingling.

Musical taste. One advantage of a DJ is having the ability to pre-select the evening's dance music. Wedding DJ's have plenty of CD's to choose from. The only consideration is the extent of the DJ's CD library. If the DJ mainly favors the top 200 party songs or whatever is currently being played on the radio, you might have a problem providing the variety that you might want. For instance, if you wanted classic rock and roll (Cream, Arrowsmith, or Led Zeppelin) thrown in with early Elvis, Chuck Berry, Jerry Lee Lewis and some Garth Brooks and the Righteous Brothers' "Unchained Melody" along with club hits like "Gettin' Jiggy With It," you might have trouble finding all of those tunes from one DJ. If you happen to thrown in some Frank Sinatra or Nat King Cole, you are really looking at quite an eclectic mix and must find a DJ with equally diverse musical taste. It can be done.

Some wedding bands cater to a variety of musical tastes, too. If you have a special request or two, some bands will even learn those songs for your reception in addition to playing your choices from those that they already have in their repertoire.

Whichever you choose, make sure that the DJ or band is flexible enough to change the song list if it isn't working. If people aren't dancing to fast tunes, then maybe the music needs to slow down a bit and let the couples get close to each other. If the slow tunes aren't bringing folks out onto the dance floor, then liven it up a bit. DJ's may have a bit more flexibility at this, but any band should have a good mix of fast and slow tunes.

Budget. Generally, DJ's usually are less expensive than a live band. However, this can vary, especially among regions. A good, but less well-known, local band can sometimes cost less than a popular DJ.

You can spend a lot of money for either a band or a DJ, or you can spend less. Whatever you do, get the best you can for the amount of money you can spend. It's been said that 80% of the success of your wedding reception depends on the entertainment. Try to budget the entertainment early on. Don't let it be just a last minute figure that you got after you had budgeted for everything else. You might find that you don't have much money left over. When you start looking for a band or DJ, you might be stuck with getting somebody less experienced or with less talent.

Some people get very wallet-conscious when a band takes a break. They feel that they aren't getting their money's worth if the band or DJ isn't playing tunes all of the time. In actuality, DJ's don't need to interrupt the music in order to take a break. They can put on a longer song or program two CD's and then take a quick trip to the bathroom or get something to drink.

Bands do need to take breaks, not only to obey the call of nature but to rest their hands and voices. Sometimes they just need to sit down for a while. The standard is a 15 minute break every hour. If you're calculating, for a four-hour reception, the band doesn't play for an hour. You will have to remember, though, that other things happen at a reception besides dancing and mingling. There are traditions that are usually sprinkled throughout the evening–the cake cutting, the toasts, the bridal toss, and the garter toss. If you have a DJ, the music will need to stop anyway. A band can always arrange their breaks to fit the reception schedule. They just need to be given a time frame or be cued by the MC.

Equipment

One thought to consider when hiring either a DJ or a live band is equipment. Find out if the DJ or band has their own equipment or must rent it. Determine exactly what their power needs will be. I've heard horror stories about bands or DJ's who were told there was so much wattage available, only to show up at the venue on the day of the reception to find that there wasn't an electrical outlet anywhere in the room and that the only power outlet was in the hallway. They had to snake in large power cables from one part of the facility to another. Not only did it look ugly but it was dangerous.

Make sure that the DJ or band visits the facility and discusses power needs with the venue. DJ's and bands know what they need, and many hotel banquet managers are very willing to discuss power and equipment needs. Banquet or hall managers may be able to refer bands and DJ's to other groups who have used the same room and worked with its acoustics and its particular power configuration. Also, the venue might also be able to help with personnel or referrals to equipment rental companies that might be able to solve a particular problem.

Another consideration is the condition of the DJ's or band's equipment. Make sure that the equipment is in good working condition. You don't want to hear hiss or buzz during the music or popping or roaring when people speak at the microphone. Find out if the band or DJ has a backup plan in case something happens to their equipment.

If it matters to you how your wedding entertainment looks, then having the night's music pour out of beat-up equipment and a small rat's nest of utility cables might distress you and your guests. If your wedding crowd is used to seeing live bands, especially local ones, then it may not be such a problem. Some usage wear is unavoidable, especially if the band or DJ tours extensively. Most music professionals take pride in the state of their equipment and will try to fix many of the more unsightly dents and dings. However, if there are offensive stickers or slogans on the bands PA equipment, you might want to either ask them to cover them during the reception or not hire the band.

Make sure that the band or DJ isn't bringing more power than the room can handle. For example, if you have booked a small banquet hall and the band starts carting in six-foot outdoor Marshal stacks, you know that your great-aunt Bertha will be blown out of her wheelchair and plastered against the back wall. Go see the band play live or ask to see the band's scrapbook. Check out their equipment and what kind of light system they use if they have one. Do this for a DJ as well.

Band

Choosing the right band can be a challenge. As we've talked about before, you need to match the band with your wedding theme, the time of day of the reception, the size of the room, and your budget. Ask your friends and relatives about good bands. Remember, though, that a band seen in a late-night bar may not have the same feel at an afternoon reception.

Draft a list of potential bands, find out where they are playing, and go listen. Ask the venue owner about the band, how reliable they are, who have they played with, and where else have they played. Look at the appearance of the band members. Will they fit in with your guests or your theme? What is the state of their equipment?

If you can't go see a band live, find out a contact number and call the band. Ask for a demo to listen to. Remember, though, that with state-of-the-art studio equipment which can blip out sour notes and wrong chords, you might be listening to quite a different band than what they are like live. Also, find out whether any band members have been replaced since the CD. Then, try to find out where they are playing and go see them live.

In your dialogue with the band, ask about experience, training, and references. Find out from their references if the band takes a lot of smoke breaks or heads for the bar at every available moment. Ask what others have done about food and beverage privileges for this particular band. Has the band abused the open bar or ate all of the leftover cake?

Find out what their band uniform is and whether they would consider more formal attire for your wedding reception. Ask if they take requests and are willing to tailor their performance to the tastes of your guests. Remember that the band usually will be playing for a wide variety of tastes and age groups.

Ask if the band would be willing to play mood music during dinner. Most bands will just play the reception dance. A few might have a small combo, comprised of two or three band members, who would be willing to do a few ballads or some light jazz while everyone eats.

Ask about price and the number of breaks the band will take. Ask if they will be willing to arrange their breaks around the events at the reception. Find out if the band expects travel expenses to be included. Usually, the band fee is a set rate. Sometimes, as a courtesy, the band is fed and offered reasonable refreshments. You want band members to enjoy themselves, but you don't want them to get totally smashed. Not only is it not professional, it is quite inappropriate around children. Make sure that the band knows this is a family occasion and not a rock concert.

Find out when the band can load into the facility. Some halls will allow the band to come in the afternoon and set up and do their sound check for the evening's wedding reception. If you are doing an afternoon reception, try to arrange to have the band come to set up well before guests arrive. Even if they do a major sound check in the afternoon, they will probably need to do a quick one before they start playing. Some bands will play a song as their sound check and have their sound man tweak things. The band and sound man will usually communicate through hand signs, then a brief word after the song to tell a band member to turn an amplifier up or down. Sometimes if everything is miked through a major board, the sound man can fine tune everything with no interruption in music, and sometimes with noone the wiser.

Ask about any illness or cancellation policy that the band has. Would the band be willing to replace performers or bring in a backup band if they couldn't make it due to breakdown or illness? Make sure you sign a detailed contract with all contingencies laid out.

DJ

Many of the considerations that you have with bands are true for DJ's. Get recommendations from friends and family, especially those recently married. Ask your caterer or reception facility for suggestions. Go to bridal showcases or wedding expos. Sometimes DJ's or bands play at these to advertise their availability. More often, though, you can get business cards at these events about DJ's and bands.

Some DJ's are part of large entertainment agencies or DJ businesses. Others are quite small one-person affairs. DJ agencies usually have lots of equipment, a vast musical library, and backup DJ's if something happens to the DJ you hired.

Smaller businesses may be able to give you more personal attention and may cost less. You will need to find out what kind of equipment they have and the size of their libraries. Also, you'll need to find out if there is backup if the DJ becomes ill. Try to avoid your cousin's teenage friend who's been spinning tunes at the local teen hangout. He wouldn't have the experience needed to handle 200+ guests and any social emergencies that might arise.

Choose three or four DJ's and make appointments to consult with them, just like you would for a band. Ask if the DJ has a recent video of a wedding to see how they interact with the crowd. Remember, though, that every wedding is different and the DJ, if he's good at what he does, will individually tailor his routine to your wishes.

Ask for references and call them. Ask about how the DJ responded to unexpected events during the evening and how he got people up dancing. Find out how long the DJ has been in business and how many wedding receptions he has done. Does the DJ have liability insurance?

Find out what their normal wedding attire is. Usually the DJ wears a tuxedo. If the men in your wedding are wearing tuxedos, then the DJ definitely should wear one. If the men are wearing suits, then a good suit would be acceptable. Make sure that the DJ isn't ultra-casual.

The next thing to consider is the size and variety of the DJ's music collection. Find out what medium it is in. Most often it's CD's, although once in awhile you will find a DJ who also travels with a turntable and vinyl records. DJ libraries can vary from 200 CD's to thousands. The average is about 1,000 CD's. Many DJ's are now using computers to play music. No matter how many CD's a DJ has, make sure that he has the variety or genre that you're looking for and the specific songs you want. Is there a variety of slow and fast songs? Are there old favorites that everyone will enjoy, including Grandma? Are there newer party songs that younger people will want to groove to when the older folks have long since gone home? Make sure you have a mix of swing, new rock, classic rock, country, hip-hop, R&B, and funk.

Find out if the DJ will play YMCA or the Macarena. In some areas, group dances like these are on the way out. In other areas, you just can't do a wedding without the Chicken Dance. If the DJ says that these dances are passe, but you and your family had a great time last month at your cousin's wedding doing the Macarena, trust your instincts. You know what music your family and friends like and what they like to do to have fun.

Bring a list of special songs when you meet with the DJ. You will need special music for some of reception events like the bridal toss and the cake cutting. You'll also want special music for the first and last dances and any other dedication dances. Find out if the DJ will take requests. Your guests may linger on the dance floor longer if they expect to hear their favorite tunes. Find out whether the DJ has his library catalogued in some way so that he can pull the songs quickly.

The next consideration is the DJ's sound system. Ask him what it is and how big it is. Make sure that the system fits the banquet room. Like a band, you don't want to overpower your quests with too much sound. And, you want to make sure that the sound is clear and without distortion, especially if the DJ is providing the microphone for the MC or is MCing himself. Some standard DJ equipment consists of four speakers, two amplifiers, two CD players, and a microphone. Usually, it is a wireless one, although some DJ's prefer to use a wireless headset.

Does the DJ have lighting equipment, mirror balls, fog machines, or other special effects equipment available? Is there an extra charge for these? How will the DJ set up the mirror ball? Will the management at the banquet facility hang it for him or does he have a lighting tree for it?

The DJ will need to set up before your guests arrive and do a sound check. Usually, this only takes thirty minutes. Have the facility manager dress the table well before the DJ arrives and locate it out of the way of the dance floor and the buffet if there is one. Make sure that the DJ is situated away from doors and doorways. You don't want someone stumbling into the DJ's equipment. Finally, make sure the DJ is facing the crowd so everyone can see what he's doing. That also makes him more available to you and your guests when you have requests or when you need to get a message to him because he's the guy with the microphone.

Finally, ask what other engagements the DJ has for the day of your reception. You don't want to have him rush through your reception just so he can make his next gig and you don't want to find out he's stuck in traffic in Timbuktu and can't set up on time.

What is the DJ's fee and what's included? Will the DJ also MC? Just how many hours will the DJ spin tunes? Will the DJ be able to offer pre-event music and dinner music, as well as dance music? Ask if the DJ has an overtime policy. Would he be willing to work an hour longer if asked? How much would it cost? Is there a cancellation policy or backup plan?

Some DJ's offer packages which include tunes and services, lights, and specialty equipment. Here are some standard ranges:

$ $400 to $1200 for four hours of music

$ $300 to $400 for lights, mirror ball, fog machine

$ $90 to $150 overtime per hour

When you have made your decision, put everything in writing in a detailed contract. Then, give the DJ a deposit. Usually this is anywhere from 10% to 60% of the fee. You may then pay the final amount the day of the reception and offer a tip at your discretion. It is a nice courtesy to offer the DJ food and beverages. But be wary of the DJ who insists he must have a clear path to the bar, however. Some DJ's make it a policy not drink all evening. After all, he's on the job.

Music Selections

One thing to remember when selecting music for your wedding reception is just how long four hours is. If you consider that the average song ranges from three minutes to five minutes, you are looking at only 50 to 80 songs. When you include breaks to cut the cake or make toasts you may be only looking at 40 to 50 songs. With that in mind, consider providing your DJ or band with only 10 to 15 favorite songs. Your wedding band may only want your dedication song list and maybe your bouquet or garter toss songs.

Don't expect your DJ or band to play a long song list straight through. For one thing, your guests will be mingling with each other, talking to you, and taking restroom breaks. They may even miss whole songs that you've so carefully chosen. Let you DJ or band judge the crowd's mood and insert a fast tune to get people out on the dance floor or put on a slow, dreamy tune to mellow out a boisterous party.

You can make your own list of songs or draw from any number of party song lists. Mobile Beat, the DJ magazine, posts a list yearly of the 200 most played party songs. You can access a copy online at www.mobilebeat.com/top200.asp. Ask your wedding band for its set list and choose your favorites from that.

Also, you might include a do not play list. There can be very good reasons for this. People may not always hear the songs they requested, because they are otherwise distracted. But, you can be sure they will always hear the song they hate.

Also, you might want to avoid further embarrassing your friends or relatives. Your Uncle Gordon may turn ape on the dance floor—and he can't dance--if he hears "Ole Time Rock 'n Roll," or Aunt Gertrude will always manage to grab a mike and sing off-key to "When a Man Loves a Woman."

* * * * * * * * * * * * *

During a wedding consultation with a couple, the bride had requested that I not play "Unchained Melody." I thought to myself, "Hey, that's odd since it's such a popular song."

At the reception, a young man came up to me and asked me to play "Unchained Melody." I looked at my Don't Play list, and there it was. I turned to the guy and said, "I do have the song, but the bride requested that I not play that particular song."

He looked at me with droopy eyes and confessed. "You know why she said that? It was our song."

I thought, "Why would you subject yourself to the torture of coming to your ex-girlfriend's wedding reception?" Yet, I saw the black humor in it. I turned to the guy and said, "Son, I guess it's not going to be an easy day for you."

* * * * * * * * * * * * *

Most of your music selections will be slow dance tunes for your dedication dances. I have a few suggestions for those special moments.

First Dance Songs

This song should be very special because it is a spotlight dance between the bride and groom, their very first dance together as a married couple. Choose a song that is special to the both of you or reflects something special about you as a couple. Most of the time, the song is slow and romantic.

I prefer something traditional like "Evergreen" by Barbara Streisand. I've had requests for "My Heat Will Go On" by Celine Dion. It's the theme from "Titanic" where the guy dies. I wonder why brides want that at their reception, but it does have a really romantic feel.

Here's a list of First Dance songs:

A Whole New World	Aladdin soundtrack
All I Ask of You	Peter Cetera and Cher
All I Have	Beth Nielsen Chapman
All I Want Is You	U2
Always	Atlantic Starr
Always and Forever	Heatwave
As Time Goes By	from Casablanca
At Last	Etta James
Babe	Styx
Baby, I Do	Natalie Cole
Beautiful	Gordon Lightfoot
Beautiful in My Eyes	Joshua Kadison
Best Thing That Ever Happened To Me	Gladys Knight
Can't Help Falling in Love	Elvis Presley
Chances Are	Johnny Mathis
Color My World	Chicago
Crazy	Patsy Cline
Crazy Love	Van Morrison
Do I Have to Say the Words	Bryan Adams
Endless Love	Lionel Richie
Everything I Do (I Do It For You)	Bryan Adams

Fairy Tale Love	Princess Bride soundtrack
Forever and Ever	Randy Travis
Groovy Kind of Love	Phil Collins
Grow Old With Me	Mary Chapin Carpenter
Have I Told You Lately	Rod Stewart or Van Morrison
Here and Now	Luther Vandross
How Sweet It Is	James Taylor
I Could Fall In Love	Selena
I Cross My Heart	George Strait (Pure Country soundtrack)
I Finally Found Someone	Bryan Adams and Barbara Streisand
If I Were You	Colin Raye
I Love the Way You Love Me	John Michael Montgomery
I'll Always Love You	Taylor Dayne
I'll Be There	Mariah Carey
In My Life	The Beatles
In Your Eyes	Peter Gabriel
Is This Love	Bob Marley
Isn't It Romantic	Frank Sinatra
It Had to Be You	Frank Sinatra
Just the Way You Are	Billy Joel
Just You and I	Eddie Rabbit and Crystal Gayle
Kiss the Girl	Little Mermaid soundtrack
Lady	John Denver
Let's Stay Together	Al Green
Maybe I'm Amazed	Paul McCartney

74

Only You	The Platters
Our Love Is Here to Stay	Harry Connick, Jr.
Someone Like You	Van Morrison
Stand By Me	Ben E. King
Still the One	Shania Twain
To Make You Feel My Love	Garth Brooks
True Companion	Mark Cohen
Truly, Madly, Deeply	Savage Garden
Try A Little Tenderness	Otis Redding
Unchained Melody	The Righteous Brothers
Unforgettable	Natalie Cole or Nat King Cole
Vision of Love	Mariah Carey
The Way You Look Tonight	Frank Sinatra or Ella Fitzgerald
Wedding Song	Paul Stookey
When I Fall In Love	Nat King Cole
When I'm With You	Sheriff
Wild is the Wind	David Bowie
Wind Beneath My Wings	Bette Midler
With You I'm Born Again	Billy Preston and Syreeta
Wonderful Tonight	Eric Clapton
You Are My Lady	Freddie Jackson
You Are So Beautiful	Joe Cocker
You Are the Sunshine of My Life	Stevie Wonder
You're All I Need to Get By	Marvin Gaye
You're the Inspiration	Chicago
You Send Me	Sam Cooke

Dedication Songs

Other dedication songs or special dances should be kept to a minimum or spread throughout the evening. By all means, the bride must dance with her father and the groom should dance with his mother. These can be done separately or together with one song tying them together like "What a Wonderful World" by Louis Armstrong. You can also have a wedding party dance where the groomsmen dance with the bridesmaids. Again, this dance doesn't have to be right at the beginning of the evening.

If there are special people that you want to dance with, go ask them some time during the wedding dance. They don't necessarily need to have a special song or to have the dance floor cleared for them. Your guests want to dance, so allow them the opportunity to do so. If they have to wait a long time to get out on the dance floor, they may leave and go somewhere else to dance.

* * * * * * * * * * * * *

At one reception I remember in particular, the bride's father had passed away and she had six brothers she wanted to recognize. She asked to have a special song for each of them. Each song was about three minutes long. So if you multiplied 6 times 3, the wedding guests had to wait an extra 18 minutes after the first dance in order to get out on the dance floor. When the dedication dances were over, it was about 25 minutes later, and people had just decided to leave. It was pretty sad, but it was what the bride wanted. She wanted to make sure she had the opportunity to dance with each of her brothers.

Here are some of the songs that are popular for dedication dances for the Bride and her father.

My Girl	The Temptations
Daddy's Little Girl	The Mills Brothers
Hero	Mariah Carey
The Men in My Little Girl's Life	Mike Douglas
My Heart Belongs to Daddy	Ella Fitzgerald
Sunrise, Sunset	Fiddler on the Roof soundtrack
Thank Heaven for Little Girls	Maurice Chevalier or Merle Haggard
The Way You Look Tonight	Frank Sinatra
You Look So Good in Love	George Strait
You Are the Sunshine of My Life	Stevie Wonder
You Are My Special Angel	Bobbie Helms

Here's a list of song suggestions for dances for the Groom and his mother.

The Greatest Love of All	Whitney Houston
If There Hadn't Been You	Billy Dean
In My Life	The Beatles
Song For My Son	Mikki Viereck
Three Times A Lady	Commodores
Through The Years	Kenny Rogers
Wind Beneath My Wings	Bette Midler
You Are So Beautiful	Joe Cocker
You've Got A Friend	James Taylor

Songs for Other Reception Events

The other events that occur at your wedding reception can be underlined if you choose special music for them. For the cake cutting, you might want "Our Love is Here to Stay" by Harry Connick, Jr. or any of the romantic First Dance songs.

For the tossing of the bouquet or garter, you might want to have a bit more fun. To toss the bouquet, you could choose "Must Be Catchin'" by Julie London or "Let's Do It" by Cole Porter. To toss the garter, I sometimes put on "The Stripper" or another fun song. You might want "She's Got Legs" by ZZ Top or "Luck Be a Lady" by Frank Sinatra.

Last Dance Song

This should be a sweetly romantic song. Almost any song from the First Dance list would be appropriate. What you want to remember is this is the last song of the evening, calling an end to the festivities and adding a beautiful note to the entire evening.

*　*　*　*　*　*　*　*　*　*　*　*　*

DECORATIONS, FAVORS, GAMES, ETC.

Hall Decorations

Decorations for the reception facility should follow your wedding theme and style. Repeat your wedding colors or shades of them in your choice of table linens, flowers, and other decorations in the room. When you chose your wedding reception venue, you already checked out the wallpaper, carpeting, and other room appointments so that they would not be glaring to your wedding style. Go back to the facility and look at the room again. Make sure that whatever colors or patterns that you use on your linens or other decorations will not clash with the decor of the room. Don't fight the existing color scheme or the patterns you find there. Work around any busy patterns and strategically place your cake table, band or DJ, buffet table, and bridal table along walls that will not clash with what you are trying to create at your reception. For example, if there is a big moose head along one wall, don't put your bridal table there or even the cake table if you can help it. You don't want Mr. Moose looking over your shoulder as you cut your cake or drink your toasts. It will look awful in your pictures. (Now, if you have an outdoorsy theme or even a medieval one, the moose head might be a nice touch.)

Also, try to look at the reception facility at the time of day in which you will hold your reception. What is the lighting like? Can you add candles or little white Christmas lights?

Are there any floral arrangements in the hall? Artificial or live potted plants or trees? Can they be moved to add some interesting touches in other parts of the room? Can you bring in screens to cover pipes or some other odd architectural or mechanical element in the room?

Finally, do you plan to bring extra flowers for the hall? You can always move some of the floral pieces from the church to the reception site, but they would have to be hand carried and set up by someone you trust. You could also have friends or relatives donate fresh cuttings from their flowering shrubs or garden flowers.

Some brides like to use helium-filled balloons as table centerpieces or in bouquets anchored to the floor to act as fillers of color. Some people use balloons to arch over a doorway or the head table or to frame a window. You can also do the same with flowers–real or silk.

Tulle netting is inexpensive and great to swirl down the center of the reception tables or to bunch up over a window or doorway. You can drape pillars with it or twist it around candelabras. You can also tie it into bows instead of more expensive satin ribbon.

Finally, you can strategically place candles of varying sizes around the room. They should be in places where they can be carefully watched, like the buffet table or the bridal table. You can also put votive candles in small containers on the reception tables, creating a romantic restaurant feel.

Table Decorations and Favors
This brings us to centerpieces and favors. Your imagination is unlimited when it comes to finding the right table

decorations for your reception. You can place little bottles of jam or cider if you are having a country wedding. You can put framed photos of the bride and groom on each table. You can display bird's nests and doves, bells, seashell soaps, seeds and seedlings or other potted plants, dried herbs or flowers, Christmas decorations for a winter wedding, floating candles, Victorian sachets, miniature sports equipment, toy cars, toy horses or other animals, bubbles, or Hershey's kisses. You can also place personalized bookmarks, notepads, magnets, chocolate roses, or personalized chocolate bars. All of these items can be customized with your names and wedding date on them.

Many people like to take something away as a souvenir of your wedding. These items can be very inexpensive, but highly personal. Some can be contracted for from custom advertizing companies. Just as you might order pencils or mugs for your company, you can order custom items for your wedding in addition to keepsake napkins with your name and wedding date. A good general rule for cost is to calculate the amount per person you are spending on food and beverages (not including the cake). Then take 9% to 12% of that figure to determine how much per person you can spend on favors or other table decorations.

Games

There has been a trend recently to include games and door prizes at wedding receptions. This has run the gamut from games to take home the centerpieces to who's going to go first to the buffet table. Others have involved games of trivia or different ways to get the bride and groom to kiss, and even pranks on the bride or groom. Some of these pranks have sometimes gotten either old or out of hand, depending on the maturity of those organizing the pranks.

Personally, I think that a wedding reception is a very dignified affair. It is a community celebration where you share the joy of being newly married with those closest to you. There are other events like wedding showers or company parties where door prizes and games have a definite place. Enjoy your friends and get out on the dance floor and have a good time.

If you want to give the centerpieces away, have someone in your wedding party give them to specific people on a list that you've drafted. That way, Aunt Julia won't leave without the centerpiece she's admired all evening. And, you will honor some other very special people in your life.

* * * * * * * * * * * * *

ORDER OF THE RECEPTION

In order for your reception to be a success, it will need to flow from one event to another without any gaps. You want to keep your guests involved in the wedding proceedings and entertained. I have found a specific order of events allows you to enjoy your guests, get the photographs you want for your wedding album, and not miss a single wedding tradition that you want to include. This simple order of events is outlined for you.

Wedding Reception Order of Events
Pre-event Activities
Introduction of Bride and Groom (No Receiving Line)
Buffet or Sit Down Dinner
Cutting the Cake
Formal Toast
Wedding Dance
    Wedding Dance–First Dance
    Wedding Dance–Music, Order, Starting the Party
Tossing the Garter and the Bouquet
Wedding Dance–End of the Evening, Last Dance
Send off

Pre-event Activities
It is very typical for people to have their wedding ceremony away from the wedding reception site. When the doors of the reception venue are opened, you usually have the staff

and wedding entertainers setting up. Many last minute details don't get placed on the tables until just before your guests arrive.

The early arrivals are quite often people who are so late to the wedding that they decided not to even go to the ceremony but headed straight to the reception. Sometimes these people are out of town guests. They should have something to do besides watch the wait staff place glasses on the tables.

The very first thing that I would recommend is that you have hors d'oeuvres and drinks available immediately. You should also have some kind of background music going for the early arrivals. This could be something your wedding DJ provides or some CD's that you have brought that the band plays. It might even be a small combo that just provides cocktail jazz or a harpist playing something romantic and airy.

Then as your ceremony ends, people who are not part of the wedding party will begin to arrive. The wedding party and both sets of parents will usually remain for photographs and the signing of the marriage license.

Your guests will come in and start to mix and mingle. They will sign the guest book and pick up table cards, if any. Remember that many of these people may never have met before, especially if the bride and groom are from different cities or states. Please make sure that you have something for them going on. Oftentimes, it will be twenty minutes to a half hour before the bride and groom grace the reception hall doors.

Introduction of Bride and Groom

During the next half hour or so, the bride and groom arrive. When this occurs, there is a formal introduction. In my order of events, there is no receiving line. The thing about receiving lines that people don't like, and probably one reason that it has gone out of fashion in many places, is the time it takes up. Granted, you have the opportunity to see everybody who came to your wedding. Unfortunately, there's always a person in the line that takes a little bit longer than everybody else. The bride and groom often run out of things to say, especially in response to such social gems as, "How'd you get here?" or "I didn't know you were getting married?" Also, your guests are stuck in line with people who have already run out of small talk. By eliminating the receiving line, you can greet your guests later during the reception itself.

You, therefore, want to make a grand entrance with your wedding party. At that time, you will be formally introduced as a married couple. This used to be fairly cut and dried: "Ladies and Gentlemen, I present to you Mr. and Mrs. John Smith." But, nowadays, it can get a little sticky. It may be "Joe Smith and Mrs. Joe Jones-Smith" or "Mr. Joe Smith and Dr. Elizabeth Jones-Smith." or even "I present to you the newly married couple: Joe Smith and Elizabeth Jones." Have your wedding MC make sure to get the introduction just right.

Also, you may want to honor the wedding party and introduce them, too. It's fairly typical when you introduce the wedding party, it will take about ten minutes or so to announce all those in line. Oftentimes, it's just the bridesmaids, the groomsmen, the maid or matron of honor, the best man, and then, of course, the bride and groom. When you get the wedding party introduced and you're about to introduce the bridal couple, your wedding MC will say, "Ladies and Gentlemen, at this time, please rise to honor the bride and groom. Let's have a big round of applause for Mr. and Mrs. Joe Smith."

You don't typically introduce the parents of the bride and groom. The main reason your don't is a practical one, especially in years past when the parents of the bride were always the wedding hosts. You need someone inside the reception hall who can lead everybody to their chairs. Have the parents of the bride and groom arrive just before the bride and groom. The bridal party will usually want to drive around the town for a little bit, honking horns, and celebrating their wedding to the world. The parents can then mix and mingle and welcome everybody. Nowadays, you may have two families that may not have grown up together, and each family may not even know the other family at all. The parents may even be from different states or counties. The friends of one family will probably not have met the friends of another. Parents are really the glue that will bring these groups together.

Also, you don't typically introduce the ushers because they come in stag. If they are introduced, it makes them targets for all of the single women to hit on them.

*　*　*　*　*　*　*　*　*　*　*　*　*

One of the things I remember most about wedding introductions was a time when I felt I had to introduce what I thought was the whole wedding party.　Fairly typical of

Spanish weddings, I was handed a long list of people. I had to introduce the whole house party, which included the bridal party, the parents, the sponsors, and important relatives. I felt like I was a butler at an old English estate introducing the social elite to the Queen. I ended up calling out the names of everybody as they arrived. Once I got the whole audience in the hall, I finally got to introduce the bride and groom.

* * * * * * * * * * * * *

Buffet or Sit down Dinner

When everyone finally is in the reception hall, it's a good time for everybody to mix and mingle. After that, you'll need to feed the people. Whether it's an afternoon event or an evening event, you need to feed your guests and relatively soon after they arrive at the reception site. Think about it. If it took everyone 30 minutes to get ready for the wedding ceremony, then they drove 30 minutes to the ceremony, enjoyed a half hour to hour wedding ceremony, and then they drove another 30 minutes to the reception hall, by the time the reception begins, they have been away from home for about two to three hours.

It's important to have hors d'oeuvres and drinks for your guests as they come in, but then have the standard meal. If it is a buffet or a sit-down dinner, serve the bride and groom first, followed by the wedding party and then the parents. It's a way to honor them, but it's also a way to get the thing done more efficiently. That's the whole objective to this plan, to honor people and to do everything that you want to do.

One advantage to serving the bride and groom first is they get the pick of the food. Sometimes, the bridal couple is so rushed or excited they don't eat anything before they come to the wedding ceremony. They may not have eaten for many hours.

Since the bride and groom eat first, they will be finished first. At that time, they'll have the opportunity to mingle with their guests. The bridal couple will be able to walk around and shake hands with all of their friends and relatives. The bride and groom can point out special relatives or friends and join them at various tables while they are still eating. By keeping the bride and groom moving, they won't get stuck talking to someone they don't know very well and don't know how to make small talk with. They'll have an opportunity to go to each table and talk with each of their guests. This accomplishes the same thing as a receiving line but is so much more pleasant for everyone. It's more like the bridal couple greeting guests in their own home.

Cutting the Cake

The only formality that needs to be done after the meal is the cake cutting. It makes perfect sense to do it after dinner, because cake is usually the desert. Now, often the cake table is the most beautiful place in the whole reception hall. Make sure that the table has been placed where there aren't any unsightly eyesores like restroom signs, fire extinguishers, or heating pipes. You want a beautiful backdrop for your treasured cake cutting photos. Therefore, when the wedding MC introduces the cutting of the cake, he will need to highlight this event by saying, "Ladies and Gentlemen, at this time we are getting ready for the cutting of the cake. So if you've brought your camera and would like a candid shot, please meet the bride and groom over by the cake table." Guests usually bring their cameras and want to get their own pictures of the bride and groom cutting the cake or dancing.

If the bride and groom have done their homework, they will have asked for special instruction from the cake baker on how to cut that first slice. Sometimes very elaborate cakes are specially constructed to handle pillared tiers or other confectionary architecture. Your baker will show you exactly where to make that first cut. Use the knife, not the cake server. Slice a small piece, slide it onto the cake server, then place it on a place. Use the knife to divide the piece into two small bites. It has been customary to smear some wedding cake on either the bride's or groom's face. That seems to make a fun picture. Make sure that a wet towel is available to wash the icing off cheeks and fingers. Please restrain yourself from having a food fight. That may be what some of your guests want to see, but you have spent a fortune on wedding attire and some of you bride's have had your makeup done professionally. Do you really want to ruin your wedding gown or pay for stain removal on the groom's tux or even ruin the makeup you've paid dearly for?

You also need to remember that the pictures aren't over after the cake has been cut. There are dance photos, the toasts, the bouquet and garter toss, and even the send off. You'll want to look just as handsome and beautiful as you did when you arrived at the reception hall. Normally, the bride gives the groom instructions about just how much messiness she'll handle. She's usually pretty clear that cake smashing is not to be tolerated.

* * * * * * * * * * * * *

I was at a wedding reception where the groom really got into smashing the cake into the bride's face. It was more than good fun. She went crying to the bathroom to clean up. I was sure that she was going to run out and have the marriage annulled right then and there. It took me twenty minutes to talk her into coming back out into the reception hall to dance the first dance.

* * * * * * * * * * * * *

Since the bridal couple is already at the cake table and it's beautifully decorated, have the photographer take the picture of wedding toast. Usually, the photographer poses the interlocking arms toast which is a terrific picture to get, but an awfully clumsy toast to do. To make this easier, have the MC ask the guests to raise their glasses. Either there will be champagne already poured at each table or people can raise whatever is handy. Stage the interlocking arms toast with just a bit of champagne in each glass and have the photo taken. Then prepare for the formal toast.

Formal Toast

The first recorded toast was in 435AD in Saxony. Once, though, the toast was literally scorched bread. When wine was hand decanted, there was often a lot of sediment left in wine casks and bottles. The French placed a piece of toast in the bottom of each wine cup to absorb the dregs and filter the wine. A competent toaster drank everything within the glass. With the toast, drinking every last drop of wine became much more enjoyable. Today, we carry on the well-wishing of toasting but without the soggy bread.

After the cake cutting, have the MC invite the best man up to the microphone to do the formal toast. This toast is almost always done by the best man, even if the best man really is a best woman. I once was at a wedding where the best man was the groom's best friend, a woman who dressed in a tuxedo for the occasion.

Sometimes, the father of the bride or groom or a close family friend who has traveled a long way will want to do an additional toast. That special toast will need to come second. The formal toast by the best man is always first. Have the MC say, "Ladies and Gentlemen, we are getting ready for the toast. Will everyone please rise." Have everybody grab their glasses and toast the bride and groom. At the end, say, "Cheers" or "Here, here." Other people may make toasts now or very brief wedding speeches. Sometimes, the maid of honor will make a toast or tell a warm story about the couple.

Make sure that the toasts are brief and appropriate. Prepare something that brings the guests together to celebrate this couple. Tell a story about the couple that tells the guests more about the love or dedication that these two newlyweds have. If you don't know what to say, you can read any number of books on wedding toasts (See the Resources section) for ideas or perhaps you want to read a favorite poem. The most moving toasts, however, come from the heart.

* * * * * * * * * * * * *

I'll never forget one toast that was a real tear jerked. This boy, about five years old, made his way up to me, using a white cane to get around with. He asked if he could say something. It was his mother's second marriage and she was marrying a man named Michael. I gave the little boy the mike, and he said very clearly, "Mommy, I love you very much. Michael, I love you too, and I can see you as my daddy." This kid's name was Joey; and he was blind. There was not a dry eye in the place as he went back to be with his mother and his new father, the man that he could see as his dad.

* * * * * * * * * * * * *

After the formal toast and the other toasts, it is a perfect time for the bride and groom to come up to the microphone and greet their guests formally. Since everyone's attention has already been focused on the microphone and where the bride and groom are, the bridal couple can address the crowd and thank them for coming. They can say something like, "You know, ladies and gentlemen, this has been a very special evening. We'd like to thank you for coming. Let's all now get ready to dance."

* * * * * * * * * * * * *

Of course, I've seen some pretty disgusting things at wedding receptions, too. I was at a wedding where two teen-agers were getting married at a very exclusive hotel. Of course, teenagers have minds of their own and band in cliques and groups. The bridal couple must have invited everyone of their friends. There were at least eight or nine bridesmaids and groomsmen on each side.

Of course, they weren't old enough to drink but they were drinking anyway. When it came time for the formal toast, the best man says, "To honor," then he raised his glass and added, "Get on her and stay on her." With that one of the other groomsmen chimed in, "Yeah, and come in her and come on her."

I just shook my head and looked pitifully at the parents. I wanted to say, "Man, you must be proud."

At that very same wedding reception, the teenagers gave out cigars, the big, fat type. This was a little while back when smoking cigars was really in vogue. These kids got to smok-ing these fat cigars as if you got a prize if you smoked it down to the end first. They were puffing on these cigars big time. You'll have to remember that this reception was at one of the most exclusive hotels in all of Houston. I'll be dam if the fire sprinklers didn't come on, soaking everyone. Now, sprinkler system water isn't regular tap water. It's grey water. We were in all tuxedos and expensive gowns and we all ended up smelling like raw sewage. That was quite a memorable night!

* * * * * * * * * * * * *

Wedding Dance–first Dance

After the toasts, it's time to start the dancing. It is customary to spotlight the bride and groom first, followed by the bride and her father, and then the groom and his mother. You can combine the parents' dances by starting with the bride and her father, and then halfway through the song have the groom and his mother join in.

Sometimes, there is a Grand March. All of the guests line up and follow a leader through the guests until the entire group is circling the bride and groom. Here then the bridal couple dances their first dance. On other occasions, the MC will call the bride and groom to the dance floor.

The first dance is a romantic dance that showcases the bride and groom. It is a dedication dance, therefore no one else dances except the bridal couple. Some wedding coordinators or even wedding entertainers advise engaged couples to take ballroom dancing lessons so that they will look terrific on the dance floor for that first dance. My advice: don't bother for this dance, unless it is something that you really want to do.

The first dance is a really another photo opportunity. You don't want to have to do a dance with fancy steps when the photographer or your Cousin Louie stops you to have that perfect dance photo. You'll lose your place and have to try to find out where you are in the dance routine to jump in again. A simple waltz or slow dance is fine.

The dedication dances for the bride and her father and the groom and his mother are other photo opportunities. If your father or mother doesn't like being in the spotlight with a lot of people watching, bow out early or invite others to join in about halfway through.

Wedding Dance

After the dedication dances are done, start off the music with something slow and fairly familiar so that everybody can come up and dance. "Ladies and gentlemen, we want to welcome everybody out to the dance floor." Do it slowly. People have just finished eating. You want to give them the opportunity to get up slowly and work out the kinks. Play something familiar that's not very hard. Make sure it's something that would be attractive to older people because they will be the first ones to leave. Some older couples really love to dance—it's often their favorite exercise together—so don't be surprised if the older crowd doesn't leave for a while.

When the majority of the older folks leave or it just gets later in the evening, you'll feel so much better about your music choices because you offered music that these family and friend seniors really liked. If they danced a lot, you know they had a good time. If they chose not to dance, you know that many of them were probably saying, "Well, you know, I didn't dance, but, by golly, I could have if I really wanted to."

You don't want them to leave saying, "Gosh, I didn't know what kind of music he was playing or from what planet!" When that happens, you know you've pushed them out the door. You want to give your older friends and relatives the opportunity to enjoy themselves a little while longer, if they want. You don't have to worry about the younger people, they will stay all night long and dance to anything.

About halfway through the evening or when the older folks leave, you can start picking it up with familiar, fast-paced music. You'll get everybody up and dancing. If you've picked some favorite music and your band or DJ is experience, everybody will get a chance to get out on the dance floor and dance.

A wedding reception is not like a club. A lot of times, people who come to wedding receptions don't get out very much. They may have not heard some of the new music, but really enjoy the standards like Frank Sinatra or Elvis. Clubs also may only play one slow song an hour. Make sure you have a slow song every 15 to 20 minutes. After all, weddings are romantic, and it makes everyone feel suave. You want to make sure you have fast songs and slow songs so that everybody in the room has the opportunity to dance.

You might also want to include a money dance of some kind. Usually called a Dollar Dance, it involves more than a dollar. Guests give money to dance with the bride. Sometimes the ladies line up and pay to dance with the groom. Some people call this the Honeymoon Dance, and it was supposed to help finance the honeymoon trip.

Tossing the Garter and the Bouquet

You want to keep the party going until about an hour before the end. At that time, you arrange for the toss of the bouquet and the garter. If you ever wanted to get silly during the evening, that is the time to do it. It's a wide angle shot. The bride's hair is all messed up. The groom doesn't even know where his tuxedo coat is.

Do the bouquet toss first because it is a bit more formal than the garter toss. Clear the dance floor and have the MC say, "Ladies and gentlemen, we are going to toss the bouquet and garter. We'd like to start by inviting the ladies out onto the dance floor." You'll notice that they'll come running. They've all had a little alcohol in them and are all caught up in the romance of the whole of idea of marriage. Ladies beat a path out to the dance floor for the bouquet toss. Have the MC get them lined up and have the bride toss the bouquet. It will be a fun time for everybody. They'll be getting silly and having a good time.

*   *   *   *   *   *   *   *   *   *   *   *   *

Once the bride's aim was really off when she tossed the bouquet and I caught it. I had to toss it back because I was already married!

Another bride tossed the bouquet once and it hit a glass and knocked it off the table. So, she tried it again and threw it in a different direction, only to knock over a pitcher. It wasn't a good night for her.

I've also seen a bride toss her bouquet, by accident, into the ceiling fan. Since the bouquet had been made a few days before, it had time to get firm. When the fan got to it, it cleanly chopped it up, allowing each of the women to get a flower out of it. There had to be some meaning in that.

Finally, I've seen where the bouquet has been tossed and then it hits the floor. All of the flowers fell off of it. So when the bride tossed it again, the lucky lady who finally caught it got only a handful of stems!

* * * * * * * * * * * * *

Once the bouquet toss is over, bring out a chair for the bride and set up the garter toss. Why is it that the single ladies are all excited about catching the bouquet, but the single men look like they're getting pushed in front of a firing squad. Although, I have seen some men collect quite a few and hang them from their rear-view mirrors.

The tossing of the garter can be a lot of fun. Once you get the guys out there and the music starts, they often get into it. Just make sure that there are still people around to enjoy it. I usually play part of "The Stripper" as the groom removes the garter.

* * * * * * * * * * * * *

Once I was working a wedding reception for two police officers who were getting married. During the garter toss, just as the groom pushed up the bride's dress, the groom found a gun in the garter! She had a right to have it as a concealed weapon, but it didn't make me feel too comfortable since it was probably loaded and so were the guests.

There was also the reception where two older people got married. The gentleman and his buddies were all senior citizens and they were getting pretty revved up later in the evening. When it came time for the garter toss, the groom's buddies kept yelling, "Teeth, teeth." And sure enough, the groom took out his dentures and put them on the garter. Who would have guessed it!

Finally, at one reception when I started playing "The Stripper" for the groom to take the garter off the bride's leg, everybody just stared at me. I wondered why they had that reaction, till someone told me that the bride really was a stripper!

＊　＊　＊　＊　＊　＊　＊　＊　＊　＊　＊　＊　＊

Wedding Dance–End of the Evening, Last Dance

After the garter is tossed, you'll want to do some more fun stuff. As long as people are feeling silly, there's no harm in cranking out some novelty songs. People like to do group dances like the Chicken Dance, the Hokey Pogey, the YMCA. Continue the good fun, dance a little while longer, and then start winding it down.

Start playing some slow music about a half hour before the end. This is the perfect time to ask that beautiful girl to dance or to feel really warm and cozy with your wife. Make sure everyone has the opportunity to spend some special moments together, not only with the bride and groom, but also with each other. Wedding receptions are perfect opportunities for families and friends to have some fun and spend some special time together. Since this is the union of two families, maybe they can even really begin to feel some closeness like family.

Let the MC call out the bride and groom to dance one last dance. This dance is a signal that not only is the event over, but the bride and groom are getting ready to start their life together. It's one last opportunity to honor the bride and groom as a couple. And from that point in time, the party ends. The bride and groom truly are the glue for the whole party. The bride's family leaves and goes over to someone's house. You'll have the groom's family go to somebody else's house and maybe have a reunion. And the college friends go somewhere else to have a little gettogether.

Send off

Once the bride and groom leave, the party is over. But there is usually one last tradition–sending off the bridal couple. Traditionally, guest threw rice after the couple. Recently, that was changed to birdseed or confetti when there was the suggestion that birds would be harmed by it. But that was also frowned on, too. I think the main object to anything being thrown at the bride was really one of cleanup.

Creative people have come up with balloon releasing and bubble blowing. Some people release butterflies or doves, but that should be done with caution. You will need to make sure that the area that you release butterflies or doves in is suitable for the butterflies or doves and for the local ecosystem. Still, other people have flown kites or rang bells. Some couples have even left under the flashes of fireworks.

As for the perfect getaway vehicle, that's really up to your individual taste and your wallet. Some couples like to ride off in a horse-drawn buggy. Some want to drift off in a colorful hot-air balloon. You can drive into the sunset in elegant sedan cars, limousines, vintage cars, or Rolls Royces. Most couples just want to speed away in any available vehicle.

Please remember if you want to decorate someone's wedding car, what you put on the finish may not come off. Putting rocks in the hub cabs is harmless and so is tying shoes or tin cans to the bumper. But the shoes or tin cans will have to be removed if the couple goes any distance. Also, make sure the car's windshield is left alone, and nothing is put in the gas tank. We want the bridal couple to have a fun sendoff, and we want them to reach their wedding hotel safely.

Well, that's it. If you follow the tips in this book, you should have a smoothly-running reception that you will be very proud of. Good luck!

Reception Checklist

Set Up

Play background music as guests arrive.

1st Hour

Meet Bride and Groom before they enter reception.

Introduce Wedding Party. ____Yes (list provided)   ____No

Introduce Bride & Groom as:

_____

Open Buffet or announce dinner service, starting with the Bride and Groom.

Continue background music while Bride and Groom eat and mingle.

2nd Hour

Announce cake cutting.

Have guests fill glasses for the formal toast.

Get Best Man (name)

_____ready for the formal toast.

Bride and Groom 1st Dance:

_____

(Title and artist)

Bride and Father Dance:

_____

(Title and artist)

Dedication to family and friends

Play lots of different music.

3rd & 4th Hours

Play fun music until Bride is ready for the bouquet and garter toss.

Party the rest of the night.
Last dance (if they want it):

_____
(Title and artist)
Have guest line up to see the Bride and Groom off.

RESOURCE LIST

MAGAZINES
Bride
Modern Bride
Bridal Guide

BOOKS
John Bowden
   Making a Wedding Speech: How to Prepare and Deliver a Confident and Memorable Address. How To Books. 1998.

Danielle Claro
   How to Have the Wedding You Want (Not the One Everybody Else Wants You to Have). New York NY: Berkley Publishing Group. 1995

Sharon Dlugosch
   Wedding Plans: 50 Unique Themes for the Wedding of Your Dreams. St. Paul MN: Brighton Publications. 1996.

Denise Fields
   Bridal Bargains: Secrets to Throwing a Fantastic Wedding on a Realistic Budget. Boulder, CO: Windsor Peak Press. 1999.
   Far and Away Weddings: Secrets to Planning a Long-Distance Wedding. Boulder CO: Windsor Peak Press. 1994.

Barbara Jeffery

Wedding Speeches and Toasts. Trans-Atlantic Press

Cindy Moore and Tricia Windom, with Martha Giddens Nesbit

Planning a Wedding with Divorced Parents. New York: Crown Publishers. 1992.

Carroll Stoner

Weddings for Grownups: Everything You Need to Know to Plan Your Wedding Your Way. San Francisco CA: Chronicle Books. 1997.

Diane Warner

How to Have a Big Wedding on a Small Budget. Cincinnati, OH: Betterway Books. 1997.

The Big Wedding on a Small Budget: Planner & Organizer. Cincinnati, OH: Writer's Digest Books. 1992.

Beautiful Wedding Decorations & Gifts on a Small Budget. F & W Publications, Inc. 1995.

Picture-Perfect Worry-Free Weddings: 72 Destinations & Venues. F & W Publications, Inc. 1998.

Diane Warner's Complete Book of Wedding Toasts Hundreds of Ways to Say 'Congratulations!' Career Press, Inc. 1997.

Dede Wilson

The Wedding Cake Book. Wiley Press. 1997.

Amusement Park Wedding Contacts
Disney World's Fairy Tale Weddings
Orlando FL
(407) 828-3400
www.disney.go.com

Disneyland's Fairy Tale Weddings
Annaheim CA
(714) 956-6527
www.disney.go.com

SeaWorld
Orlando Fl
(407) 363-2273
www.seaworld.com

Busch Gardens
Tampa FL
(813) 987-5209
www.buschgardens.com

Knotts Berry Farm
Buena Park CA
(714) 243-2028
www.knots.com/Catering/catering.htm

Dollywood
Pigeon Forge TN
(423) 428-9488
www.dollywood.com

Dutch Wonderland
E. Lancaster PA
(717) 534-4900
www.dutchwonderland.com

Hershey Chocolate World
Hershey PA
(717) 534-4900
www.hersheys.com/chocworld

Mall of America, Chapel of Love
Minneapolis MN
(800) 299-LOVE
www.mlonda@chapeloflove.com

Six Flags Over Texas
Arlington TX
(817) 640-8900
www.sixflags.com